Essential Guide for Supply Chain Management using Microsoft Dynamics AX

2016 Edition

Other Books by Scott Hamilton

Supply Chain Management Using Microsoft Dynamics AX: 2016 Edition, Visions, Inc. (2016)

Process Manufacturing Using Microsoft Dynamics AS: 2016 Edition, Visions, Inc. (2016)

Warehouse Management Using Microsoft Dynamics AX: 2016 Edition, Visions, Inc. (2016)

Discrete Manufacturing Using Microsoft Dynamics AX 2012, Visions Inc. (2012)

Food Products Manufacturing Using Microsoft Dynamics AX 2012, Visions Inc. (2012)

Managing Process Manufacturing Using Microsoft Dynamics AX 2009, Visions Inc. (2010)

Managing Wholesale Distribution Using Microsoft Dynamics AX 2009, privately published (2010)

Managing Lean Manufacturing Using Microsoft Dynamics AX 2009, Visions Inc. (2010)

Managing Your Supply Chain Using Microsoft Dynamics AX 2009, Printing Arts (2009)

Managing Your Supply Chain Using Microsoft Dynamics AX 4.0, Printing Arts (2007)

Managing Your Supply Chain Using Microsoft Axapta 3.0, McGraw-Hill (2004)

Managing Your Supply Chain Using Microsoft Navision, McGraw-Hill (2004)

Maximizing Your ERP System, McGraw-Hill (2003)

Managing Information: How Information Systems Impact Organizational Strategy (with Gordon B. Davis), Business One Irwin (1993)

Scott Hamilton, Ph.D.

eBook ISBN 978-0-9884976-9-6
Print ISBN 978-0-9884976-0-3

The front cover photo depicts the waves on the north coast of Kauai in Hawaii, and was taken by the nationally-recognized photographer Doug Peck (www.douglaspeckphotography.com).

Preface

This book focuses on how Microsoft Dynamics AX supports supply chain management (SCM) in manufacturing and distribution businesses. It provides an overview of the most critical capabilities and business processes, and presents a linear sequence of topics that build on each other. The targeted reader consists of SCM professionals that need to initially learn AX.

As an Essential Guide, it represents an abbreviated version of my complete book for "Supply Chain Management using Microsoft Dynamics AX: 2016 Edition". It focuses on topics that apply to both distribution and manufacturing, but skims over the manufacturing-related topics due to book length considerations. These topics are covered in the complete book.

The book contents cover two major options currently available for using AX, which can be labeled "Dynamics AX 2012 R3" and the "new Dynamics AX". The two options provide the same supply chain management functionality with some slight differences, so that the book contents apply to both options. The book identifies the slight differences such as the variations in user experience and the workspace capabilities. Beneath these look and feel changes, the two options share the same embedded conceptual models and business processes.

Four previous books similarly focused on supply chain management using AX, especially for discrete manufacturing/distribution businesses. Each previous book covered a major software version but they could just as easily been titled different editions. The first three books were titled *Managing Your Supply Chain*, and they represented the 2004 Edition (for AX 3.0), the 2007 Edition (for AX 4.0), and the 2009 Edition (for AX 2009). The fourth book was titled slightly differently to indicate the focus on SCM in Discrete Manufacturing, and it represented the 2012 Edition (for AX 2012). In addition, three previous books covered SCM for the process industries, including the latest book *Process Manufacturing using Microsoft Dynamics AX: 2016 Edition.*

A trail guide and topographic maps provide essential information when exploring any unknown territory. They identify the most important features of the landscape and provide insights about key considerations and trail variations. Similar essentials apply to those exploring the use of an ERP system to run their business. As a trail guide, this book identifies the most important features of the embedded conceptual models and business processes related to supply chain management using AX, and provides insights about key considerations and variations.

Many people helped in completing this book. They included Deb Skoog, Elise Kling Marty and Sandra Krzyzaniak in preparing the book. In addition, many people contributed insights and feedback to the previous books which acted as the source material for this Essential Guide.

The book reflects my interpretation of how to use Microsoft Dynamics AX. Errors of omission and commission, and any misunderstandings, are hopefully minimized.[1] Corrections and suggestions are welcome, as well as additional case study examples. Please send to **ScottHamiltonPhD@aol.com**.

Each day of writing was started with the following prayer:

> Creator of all things, give me a sharp sense of understanding, a retentive memory, and the ability to grasp things correctly and fundamentally. Grant me the talent of being exact in my explanations, and the ability to express myself with thoroughness and charm. Point out the beginning, direct the progress, and help in the completion.

[1] The book is for information purposes only. The author, publisher and Microsoft make no warranties, expressed or implied, in the presentation of information.

Contents

Chapter 1

Introduction

A primary challenge for many manufacturing and distribution firms involves effective implementation and use of an ERP system for managing their supply chain. Learning the capabilities of your ERP system provides a foundation for effective usage, and re-thinking previous ways of doing business. When initially learning an ERP system, the sheer amount of functionality can be daunting, and make the task difficult and time-consuming. The learning curve can be shortened with a guide book that covers the most critical topics and processes for running the business. A guide book can help you learn the vocabulary about embedded conceptual models, and enhance the hands-on experience of system usage and navigational details. Each ERP system has its own vocabulary, conceptual models and navigational details, including Microsoft Dynamics AX.[1]

This book focuses on how Dynamics AX supports supply chain management (SCM) in manufacturing and distribution businesses. The targeted reader consists of SCM professionals that need to initially learn AX. It provides an overview of the essential business processes and capabilities, and presents a linear sequence of topics that build on each other. It covers the embedded conceptual models that ultimately shape your vocabulary for describing system usage.

As an Essential Guide, it represents an abbreviated version of my complete book for "Supply Chain Management using Microsoft Dynamics AX: 2016 Edition". It focuses on topics that apply to both distribution and manufacturing, but skims over the manufacturing-related topics due to book length considerations. These topics are covered in the complete book.

The book contents cover two major options currently available for using AX, which can be labeled "Dynamics AX 2012 R3" and the "new Dynamics AX". The two options provide the same supply chain management functionality with some slight differences, so that the book contents apply to both options. The

[1] Dynamics AX is a registered trademark of Microsoft. This book employs the term "AX" for short.

book identifies the slight differences such as the variations in user experience and the workspace capabilities. Beneath these look and feel changes, the two options share the same embedded conceptual models and business processes.

This chapter starts with suggestions for the targeted reader, and describes the scope of book topics. It also covers several aspects of terminology and highlights the use of business process modeling (BPM) diagrams as a learning tool. These considerations are reflected in the following sections within this chapter.

1. Suggestions for the Targeted Reader
2. Scope of Book Topics and Prior Research
3. Terminology Used in the Book
4. Variations in the User Experience and the Use of Workspaces
5. Business Process Modeling (BPM) Diagrams as Learning Tools
6. Baseline Model of Operations
7. Summary of Case Studies

1.1 Suggestions for the Targeted Reader

The targeted reader consists of SCM professionals that need to initially learn Dynamics AX for running a distribution/manufacturing business. In many cases, they comprise the project team responsible for the initial implementation. In other cases, they may need to learn AX because of a change in positions or job responsibilities. Prospective users (and AX consultants) may also want to initially learn AX. In addition, many people with some AX experience may want to confirm and extend their AX knowledge, or selectively learn a topic. Figure 1.1 summarizes these learning objectives.

Figure 1.1 Suggestions for the Targeted Reader

Learning Objective	Estimated Pages
Initially Learn AX	100-130
Extend/Confirm existing AX knowledge	
Selectively Learn AX Capabilities	

The objective to initially learn AX can benefit from an overview of the essential business processes and capabilities, especially in a linear sequence of topics that build on each other. The linear sequence starts with the fundamentals of modeling inventory locations and the definition of material items, including the basics of product costing. The sequence continues with the definition of coverage planning data to model SCM decision-making, and an overview of S&OP game plans and the use of master scheduling logic to coordinate supply chain activities. Subsequent chapters cover the key business processes related to sales orders, purchase orders, and transfer orders, and some basic aspects of warehouse management and quality management. The book chapters reflect this linear sequence, as shown in Figure 1.2.

Figure 1.2 Organization of Book Chapters

Chapter	Foundation Topics
2	Modeling Inventory Locations
3	Definition of a Material Item
4	Product Costing
5	Coverage Planning Data to Model SCM Decision-Making

Key Business Processes	Chapter
Sales Order Processing	7
Purchase Order Processing	8
Transfer Order Processing	9
Inventory & Warehouse Management	10

Chapter	Sales & Operations Planning
6	S&OP and Master Scheduling

Additional Topics	Chapter
Quality Management	11

Many of the chapters start with a basic business process that reflects the key constructs and embedded conceptual models within AX. The typical steps and role responsibilities are illustrated using BPM diagrams. The basic process provides a baseline for explaining key considerations and variations, thereby supporting a "+1" learning approach.

1.2 Scope of Book Topics and Prior Research

This Essential Guide focuses on supply chain management topics that apply to distribution and manufacturing companies. It skims over or excludes several manufacturing-related topics because of book length considerations, and these topics are covered in the complete book.[2] It also skims over or excludes several

[2] The excluded topics related to manufacturing involve bills of material, production resources and routings, cost calculations for manufactured items, planning data and S&OP game plans for manufactured items, production orders, subcontracted production, and configuration technologies for custom product manufacturing.

other topics for the same reason, as described in Appendix A about the scope of book topics. This appendix also describes the scope of prior research.

The selection of topics for this essential guide were shaped by my experience in teaching SCM professionals across the past three decades. This includes teaching new users (and experienced users) as part of consulting engagements with several hundred firms, and also teaching SCM topics as part of executive seminars, APICS certification classes, MBA courses, user group sessions, and AX training courses. The topics were also shaped by my experience in writing multiple books about SCM using AX.

1.3 Terminology Used in the Book

The terminology associated with many aspects of supply chain management can vary widely between companies and ERP systems. It is often difficult to clearly understand the meaning of a term -- such as inventory status, reservations, shipments, work orders, and sales or purchase agreements -- without a lengthy discussion about its significance.

As much as possible, this book consistently uses the same terminology to describe the conceptual models and software functionality within AX. In most cases, the book's terminology reflects the names employed by the AX software, such as the names of forms and fields. However, it sometimes reflects generally accepted terms or alternative phrasing to clarify understanding.

One difficulty in terminology stems from the book's attempt to explain two different options for using AX, consisting of AX 2012 R3 version and the new Dynamics AX. The embedded conceptual models and business processes within the two options are fundamentally the same for supply chain management topics, but there are slight changes. A comprehensive list of these changes was not available prior to book publications. The book uses the new term when known, otherwise it uses the terminology from AX 2012 R3.

1.4 Variations in the User Experience and the Use of Workspaces

This book focuses on the embedded conceptual models and business processes within standard AX. The user experience and navigational details may differ -- whether using customized forms, workspaces, web-based applications, or hand-held devices -- but the embedded conceptual models and business processes still apply. This section summarizes the variations in user experience and the use of workspaces.

Variations of the User Experience The standard menu structure and user-defined favorites provide commonly used approaches for navigation. When using the new Dynamics AX, the links within workspaces provide another approach for navigating to commonly used tasks. An additional approach – termed "search for a page" – enables you to specify the desired topic, review a list of applicable forms, and then navigate to a selected form.

Use of Workspaces Workspaces represent one variation in the user experience when using the new Dynamics AX.[3] Workspaces provide an aggregation of tasks related to a specific role. Almost half of the 30+ currently available workspaces apply to the SCM-related topics within the book, as summarized in Figure 1.3. Separate sections describe the workspaces related to item definition (Section 3.14), master scheduling (Section 6.7), sales orders (Section 7.7), purchase orders (Section 8.9), and warehouse management (Section 10.6).

Figure 1.3 Examples of SCM-Related Workspaces

Design	Released Product Maintenance Product Readiness Cost Administration Product Variant Model Definition
Sell	Sales Order Processing & Inquiry Sales Return Processing
Procure	Purchase Order Preparation Purchase Order Receipt & Follow-up
S&OP	Master Planning
Produce	Production Floor Management
Warehouse	Outbound Work Planning Outbound Work Monitoring Cost Administration Cost Analysis

1.5 Business Process Modeling (BPM) Diagrams as a Learning Tool

One of the book's primary objectives consists of learning the embedded conceptual models and business processes within standard AX. In many implementations, these business processes can help the project team gain an

[3] The workspace functionality replaces several capabilities in AX 2012 R3, such as role-centered pages and the employee portal. The role-centered pages were built on the deprecated Enterprise Portal capabilities which have been replaced by the new web client platform. The new platform supports the use of workspaces - and the related definition of workspace patterns to support different devices - for navigating to commonly used tasks. For example, a workspace pattern can be specified for a list page, where the number of displayed columns needs to reflect the size of the device.

overall understanding of system usage and each team member's roles, enabling them to envision new business practices and the real need for customizations. Many of the chapters include Business Process Modeling (BPM) diagrams about basic business processes. These basic processes provide the foundation for more extended explanations and for covering major variations. BPM diagrams are primarily used as a learning tool within this book, and my diagrams do not adhere exactly to the BPM standards. The diagrams employ a limited number of symbols to keep things simple. For example, three symbols are used to denote "And", "Or" and "Any, None, or All". A fourth symbol for an "Event" indicates an automatic action within AX, which helps explain some of the behind-the-scenes functionality. The BPM diagrams indicate a sub-process using a bold border for the activity.

1.6 Baseline Model of Operations

A baseline model of operations represents the common use of Dynamics AX and dominant business practices within many manufacturing and distribution businesses. It provides a foundation for simplified explanations about how to use Dynamics AX to manage the business, and for explaining variations to the baseline model. In summary, the baseline model focuses on a single AX company with one or more AX sites (and their related AX warehouses) with standard products identified by an item number. Inventory is tracked by site, warehouse and bin location, with inventory replenishment logic at the site/warehouse level. Sales prices and purchase prices are typically companywide, although they can optionally reflect site- or warehouse-specific prices. Each manufactured item requires bill of material information, with optional definition of routing data. The following points provide more detailed explanations about the baseline model of operations.

Single Company and AX instance The baseline model consists of a single company using a single AX instance. Some scenarios involve multiple companies within one instance and possible partitioning of these companies within the database. A multicompany supply chain is treated as a variation to the baseline model.

Multiple Inventory Locations Identified by an AX site and AX Warehouse Each physical location is typically identified by an AX site and an associated value for a "site" financial dimension. The site-specific financial dimension supports financial reports by site. Each AX site has one or more AX warehouses. Each AX warehouse has one or more bin locations, although use of bin locations is not mandatory. The definition and use of warehouse locations differ significantly between the basic and advanced approach to warehouse management.

Material Items Identified by Item Number Material items are identified by an item number. In some cases, an item may be identified by an item number and one or more additional fields termed variant codes, as illustrated in Case 3.3. In other cases, a product configurator can result in the creation of a configuration ID for the item number. These are treated as variations to the baseline model of operations.

Bill of Material and Routing for a Manufactured Item A bill of material (BOM) defines the product structure for a manufactured item. Alternatively, the product structure can be defined by a formula, especially in process-oriented operations). Many scenarios will also define production resources and routings for manufactured items, but it is optional. As already noted, an explanation of these manufacturing-related topics falls outside the scope of this essential guide.

Standard or Actual Costing for Material Items Each material item must be assigned an inventory valuation method reflecting a standard cost or actual cost method. With standard costing, a costing version must be defined for standard costs, and each material item must have an item cost record for each site with inventory.

Inventory Replenishment Logic Applies to the Site/Warehouse Level Replenishment logic is defined by an item's coverage planning data, and applies to the site/warehouse level. In some cases, the logic may only apply to the site.

Batch and/or Serial Numbers for a Material Item The use of batch and/or serial numbers is treated as a variation to the baseline model.

1.7 Summary of Case Studies

Case studies illustrate how the AX software functionality applies to many different scenarios in manufacturing and distribution. Each chapter includes case studies applicable to the topic, and a complete list of case studies is provided at the end of the book. Additional case studies are included in the complete book.

Chapter 2

Fundamentals of Modeling Inventory Locations

The definition of physical sites containing inventory represents a key part of modeling any supply chain, and there are several fundamental options for modeling these sites within AX. These options involve the use of AX sites and AX warehouses within a legal entity. In this book, we will use the generic term of *physical site* or *inventory location* for conceptual explanations, and the terms *AX site* and *AX warehouse* when explaining system-specific functionality. In addition, we will use the term *bin location* when referring to the locations within an AX warehouse.

The model of inventory locations has multiple impacts. It impacts the definition of items, product costs, coverage planning data and S&OP game plans. In manufacturing scenarios, it impacts the definition of bills of material, production resources and routings, and the calculated costs for manufactured items. It also impacts the business processes related to inventory, such as sales orders, purchase orders, transfer orders and production orders. These impacts are covered throughout the book, and a subsequent chapter provides more detailed explanations about inventory and warehouse management. However, the fundamental options for modeling inventory locations are introduced now, and the chapter consists of the following sections.

1. Variations of Modeling Inventory Locations
2. Unique Considerations about using AX Sites
3. Unique Considerations about AX Warehouses

A graphical portrayal of the inventory locations – termed the operations infrastructure – identifies the multi-level structure of AX warehouses within AX sites and legal entities.

2.1 Variations for Modeling Inventory Locations

The wide variety of scenarios for supply chain management can be distilled into a few major variations for modeling inventory locations within AX. Several key factors differentiate the nature of these variations, such as the number of AX instances, the number of legal entities related to the inventory locations, and the AX approach for modeling an inventory location. Another key factor involves the need for transfers between inventory locations and the solution approach for coordinating transfers. The most common variations and the key factors are summarized in Figure 2.1 and described below.

Figure 2.1 Major Variations for Modeling Inventory Locations

		Major Variations		
		#1	#2	#3
		Autonomous Sites Without Transfers	Multiple Sites With Transfers	Multicompany Supply Chain
Key Factors	Number of AX Instances and Partitions	One		
	Number of Companies (Legal Entities)	One		Multiple
	AX Approach for Modeling an Inventory Location	Considerations about using an AX Site and AX Warehouse for Modeling an Inventory Location		
	Need for Transfers Between Inventory Locations	No	Yes	
AX Solution Approach for Coordinating Material Transfers		N/A	Transfer Orders	Intercompany Purchase Orders & Sales Orders

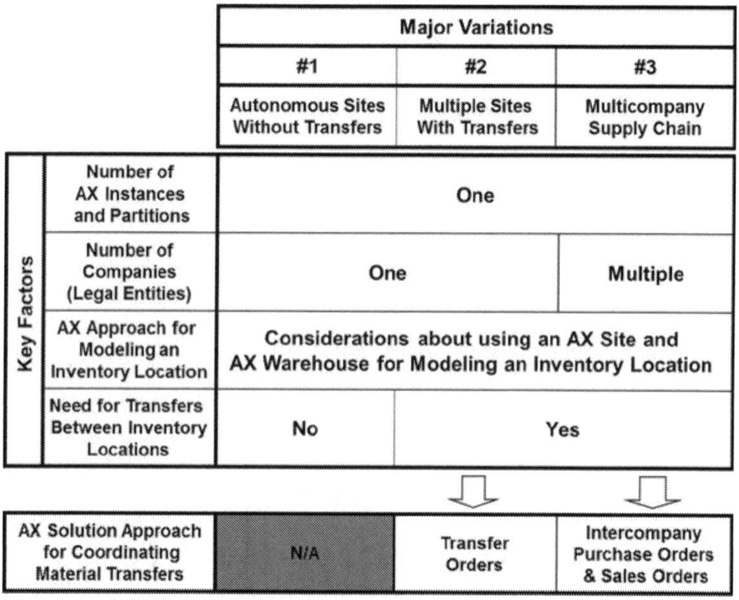

The simplest variation consists of a single AX instance and partition, and a single legal entity with one or more inventory locations. The locations may reflect autonomous sites without transfers, or they may reflect a distribution network with transfers between locations. The AX solution approach employs transfer orders for coordinating transfers between sites in the same company, and intercompany orders for transfers between sites in different companies.

All of these variations involve several considerations about using AX sites and AX warehouses for modeling inventory locations. As one example, an item's sales price can be site-specific or companywide (Section 3.4).

Several variations represent less common scenarios and are not included in Figure 2.1. For example, a given enterprise may employ two or more AX instances, where intercompany trade between locations in each instance can be handled by the Data Import/Export capabilities within AX.[1] The same capabilities also apply to intercompany trade when one of the companies employs a different ERP system than AX. A single instance can also be partitioned with one or more companies in a partition, thereby isolating the information as if separate instances were being used. These other variations fall outside the book's scope.

2.2 Unique Considerations about using AX Sites

Each physical site is typically modeled as an AX site with one or more AX warehouses. An AX site has several unique aspects that are not applicable to an AX warehouse, as summarized below.

Financial Reporting by AX Site Each AX site can have an associated value for a "site" financial dimension, thereby supporting profit and loss statements by site.

Site-Specific Standard Costs for an Item The assignment of an item's standard cost can vary by AX site. Stated another way, each material item must have an item cost record for each site with inventory. An item can have a zero value for its standard cost at a given AX site.

Site-Specific Policies for Quality Orders The automatic generation of quality orders within a business process -- such as production or purchase receiving -- provides a key tool for quality management. These policies can be site-specific or companywide.

Considerations for Manufacturing Scenarios Several considerations only apply to manufacturing scenarios, as summarized below.

- *Site-Specific BOM and Routing Information for a Manufactured Item.* The BOM and routing information for manufactured items can vary by AX site.
- *Warehouse Source of BOM Components.* The warehouse source for components and the destination warehouse for the item's production order must be within the same AX site.

---

[1] The Data Import/Export framework replaces the Application Integration Framework (AIF) capabilities in previous AX versions such as AX 2012 R3.

- *Site-Specific Labor Rates and Overhead Rates.* Labor rates and overhead costs can vary by AX site.
- *Production Resources within an AX Site.* An AX site is assigned to a resource group and its related resources.

2.3 Unique Considerations about AX Warehouses

Each physical site is typically modeled as an AX site with one or more AX warehouses, as noted in the previous section. The assignment of an AX warehouse to an AX site cannot be changed after posting inventory transactions for the warehouse, so that the initial assignments must be carefully considered. Several unique aspects apply to AX warehouses.

Use of the Basic versus Advanced Approach to Warehouse Management The choice between the basic and advanced approach to warehouse management can be warehouse-specific, and a subsequent chapter provides more detailed explanation about these options (Section 10.1). The two different approaches have different conceptual models for managing inventory. Examples of these differences include the definition of bin locations within a warehouse, the use of reservation logic, and the impact on business processes involving inventory such as sales orders, purchase orders and transfer orders.

Significance of a Transit Warehouse The need for a transit warehouse only applies when using transfer orders, so that you can track the in-transit inventory. You designate a transit warehouse when creating it, and assign a transit warehouse to each ship-from warehouse.

2.4 Additional Case Studies

Case 2.1: Modeling a Multisite and Multicompany Supply Chain A global manufacturing/distribution business consisted of multiple physical sites and transfers between sites, where some sites reflected different legal entities. As shown in Figure 2.2, a simplified example consists of the US company (with a manufacturing site and a distribution site) and the UK company (with a small distribution site). The typical Product #1 was produced at the manufacturing site, which employed several AX warehouses to track inventory of raw material, intermediates and finished goods. An additional in-transit warehouse was used to track inventory sent via transfer orders to the US distribution site, which stocked the product (based on demand forecasts) and sold it to domestic customers. The advanced approach to warehouse management was employed within the warehouses at both sites.

Figure 2.2 Modeling a Multisite and Multicompany Supply Chain

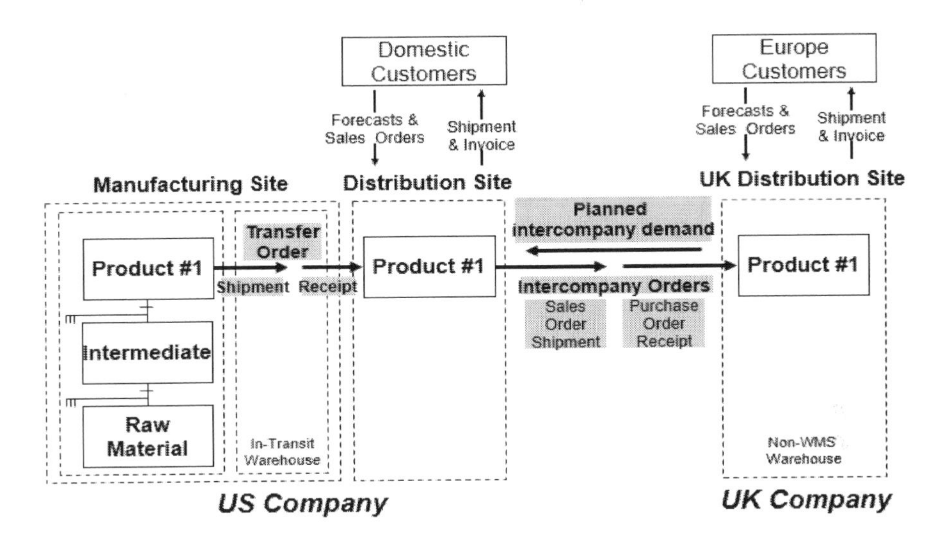

A small proportion of the product was also stocked at the UK distribution site (based on demand forecasts) and sold to European customers. These requirements were communicated to the US company as planned intercompany demand generated by master scheduling logic. Subsequent intercompany purchase orders (placed by the UK company) automatically created intercompany sales orders (for the distribution site within the US company). The transfer was reported as a sales order shipment and a purchase order receipt, and the in-transit inventory was tracked. The small UK operation was modeled as a non-WMS warehouse, and employed the basic approach to warehouse management.

Case 2.2: Modeling a Supply Chain with Subcontracted Production

A distribution company considered themselves to be a virtual manufacturer, since all production was handled by subcontractors. Some products were purchased complete. Others were produced at the subcontractor using supplied material. In the simplified example shown in Figure 2.3, Product #2 was produced at subcontractor ABC using supplied material and then transferred to the distribution warehouse. The bill of material for Product #2 identified the supplied components, and purchases of these items were delivered to the subcontractor location. The bill of material also included a component representing the "Subcontracted Service for Product #2," which reflects the AX approach to modeling subcontracted production. This item defines the value-added costs for the subcontracted service, and provides the basis for approved vendors and purchase price agreements. In addition, the purchase order for this subcontracted service is generated by and directly linked to the production order for the parent item. Hence, subcontracted production involves the dual constructs of a production order and its associated purchase order, as shown in the left side of Figure 2.3.

Figure 2.3 Modeling a Supply Chain with Subcontracted Production

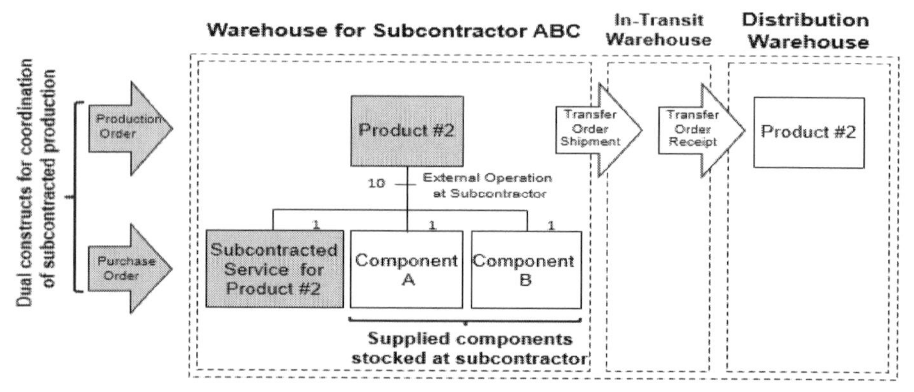

In this example, each subcontractor location was defined as a non-WMS warehouse, the distribution center was defined as a WMS-enabled warehouse, and all of these warehouses were assigned to a single AX site. As a result, the basic approach to warehouse management was used to report inventory transactions at the subcontractor locations (such as purchase order receipts and transfer order shipments) and the advanced approach was used at the distribution center.

2.5 Executive Summary

The definition of inventory locations represents a key part of modeling any supply chain, and there are several fundamental options for modeling these locations within AX. These options include the use of AX sites and AX warehouses to model inventory locations, and use of the basic versus advanced approach to warehouse management at a given AX warehouse. This chapter reviewed the major variations for modeling inventory locations, and highlighted several considerations about using AX sites and AX warehouses. The case studies illustrated how to model a supply chain with multiple sites and with subcontracted production. The fundamental options are introduced at the beginning of the book because they have multiple impacts described in subsequent chapters.

Chapter 3

Definition of a Material Item

Information about material items provides the foundation for managing supply chain activities in distribution and manufacturing environments. A comprehensive common database about item information must satisfy requirements stemming from multiple stakeholders to avoid the problems associated with multiple nonintegrated files. The stakeholders include sales, purchasing, warehouse management, quality and accounting, as well as engineering and production for manufactured items. Other stakeholder considerations include customers, vendors, industry standards, intercompany coordination, international operations and web-based applications. The multiple stakeholders often have differing requirements concerning the definition of an item.

This explanation focuses on material items identified by an item number. In AX terminology, this means you initially define each item by assigning a Product Type of *Item* and a Product Subtype of *Product*, which indicates the item identifier consists of just an item number. In addition, each item must be treated as a stocked product based on a policy within the Item Model Group assigned to the item.

A typical business process to define a material item provides a starting point for explaining key aspects of item information. The typical process requires an understanding of enterprise- versus company-level information about an item. Key aspects include the significance of the storage dimension group assigned to an item, the use of item templates, considerations about descriptive information and units of measure, and the companywide versus site- and warehouse-specific information for an item. These topics are reflected in the following sections within this chapter.

1. Enterprise- versus Company-Level Information for an Item
2. Typical Business Process to Define a Material Item
3. Essential Data for using a New Item within AX
4. Significance of the Storage Dimension Group for an Item
5. Significance of the Tracking Dimension Group for an Item
6. Using Templates for Partially Populating Item Information
7. Descriptive Information about an Item
8. Unit of Measure Considerations for an Item
9. Additional Information for a Purchased Item
10. Additional Information for a Manufactured Item
11. Additional Information for a Salable Item
12. Company versus Site/Warehouse Information for an Item
13. Inventory Costing and Financial Reporting for Items
14. Workspaces Related to Item Definition

3.1 Enterprise- versus Company-Level Information for an Item

The business process for defining a material item requires an understanding of enterprise-level versus company-level information within AX, whether you manage one or multiple companies within an AX instance. In summary, the concept of enterprise- versus company-level information has been implemented within AX using two different constructs and their identifiers -- termed the product number and the item number. The product number provides a unique identifier for enterprise-level information about products, whereas the item number provides the unique identifier for company-level information about items. A subset of information is defined at the enterprise level, such as the product name, product category and several key policies, whereas all other item information is defined at the company level. Two key forms are employed to maintain product and item information: the Products form (for product information) and the Released Products form (for item information).

Enterprise-Level Information for an Item In addition to the designated Product Type (of *Item*) and Product Subtype (of *Product*), key aspects of enterprise-level information include the product number, the product name and extended description (and their translations if applicable), and unit of measure conversions (if applicable).

Two Approaches for Defining an Item The conceptual model of enterprise- versus company-level information gives rise to two different approaches for defining items, termed the multi-company approach and the single-company approach.

- *Multi-company approach to defining items.* You employ a two-step process to initially define a product and then release the product to a selected company. Releasing the product creates an item number that matches the product number, and you maintain the company-level information for the item number. You can apply a template to partially populate the item information.

  As an example, a given item may be manufactured in one company and sold to a sister company that represents a distribution operation, so that the product needs to be released to two different companies. The multi-company approach supports the concept of a centralized engineering function, where centralized engineering may apply to one or more companies.

- *Single-company approach to defining items.* You employ a one-step process to simultaneously create product and item information, which automatically releases the product to the company. The one-step process allows you to specify a template (to partially populate the item information) when initially defining the item, or to apply a template later. This one-step approach can also be used in a multi-company environment to initially create a product and auto-release it to one company.

The identifiers for a product number and item number are typically assigned the same value. For example, releasing a product to a selected company automatically creates an item number that matches the product number. The one-step process also supports the assignment of the same identifier. If needed, you can optionally override the item number for a company, thereby supporting a company-specific identifier.[1] Deleting an item number from a company simply removes its authorization for the company; it does not delete the product number.

3.2 Typical Process to Define a Material Item

The business process for defining a material item requires an understanding of enterprise-level versus company-level information within AX, as described in the previous section. The conceptual model of enterprise- versus company-level

[1] You can override a different value for the item number (after it has been released to a company) using the rename capability, or when creating an item number and product number using the single-company approach.

information gives rise to two different approaches for defining a material item, termed the multi-company approach and the single-company approach. Both approaches are included in the typical business process to define a material item. The business process starts with a request for a new item, where a product designer role typically has the responsibility for initially defining the product and item information. The process ends with the approval of the new item. The steps within the business process are summarized in Figure 3.1 and described below.

Figure 3.1 Typical Process to Define a Material Item

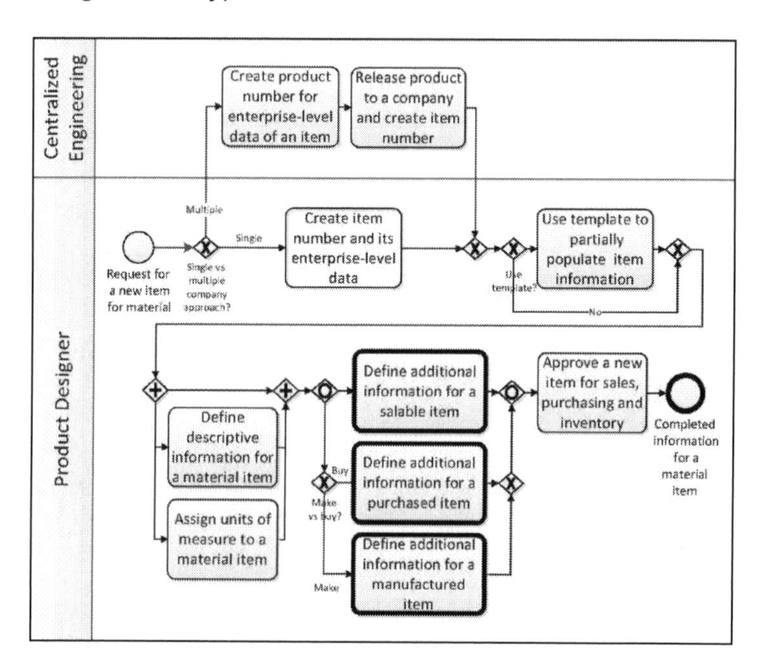

Create a Product Number and Define Enterprise-Level Data for an Item In a multicompany approach, the product designer within a centralized engineering group initially creates a product number and defines its enterprise-level data. The enterprise-level data includes the product name, extended description and several other policies. Specifying the policies about batch/serial tracking (aka the Tracking Dimension Group) and the Storage Dimension Group means they are mandated for all authorized companies.

Release a Product to a Company and Create Item Number In a multi-company approach, the product designer within a centralized engineering group releases selected product numbers to one or more companies, which automatically creates the item number within each company. After the release step, the product designer (within the local company) assigns several essential fields and other roles have the responsibility for completing additional information.

Create Item Number and Define its Enterprise-Level Data The product designer employs a single-company approach to create a new item number and define its enterprise-level data. A template may be specified when creating an item in order to partially populate item information.

Use template to partially populate item information The product designer employs a template as a short-cut approach to partially populate item information, either when creating a new item or by applying it afterward. The product designer creates a template from an existing item number, and designates it as a personal or shared template.

Define descriptive information for an item The product designer defines the item's description (and an extended description) as part of its enterprise-level information. Language-specific translations can also be defined. The descriptive information may also include documents, such as notes, Word files or other file formats.

Assign units of measure to an item The product designer assigns the inventory unit of measure (UM) to an item. The item's inventory UM is used to display inventory balances, define costs, and calculate replenishment. An item may have additional units of measure for purchasing, sales or warehouse purposes, which may require item-specific UM conversion factors with the item's inventory UM.

Define additional information for a salable item The sales manager defines the sales pricing and possible discounts for a saleable item. The sales manager may also define sales agreements, the applicable product category, and the start dates for selling and shipping a new product.

Define additional information for a purchased item The definition of information for a purchased item involves several activities performed by different roles. The purchasing agent defines an item's approved vendors, purchase prices and planning data. The accounting manager defines the item's accounting information and inventory valuation method (standard versus actual cost), and the cost accountant defines an item's standard cost. If applicable, the quality control manager defines the item's testing requirements and the policies for batch and/or serial tracking.

Define additional information for a manufactured item The definition of information for a manufactured item involves several activities performed by different roles. The product designer defines an item's bill of material. The process engineer defines the routing for an item. The production planner defines the item's planning data. The accounting manager defines the item's accounting information and inventory valuation method (standard versus actual cost), and the cost accountant calculates the cost of a manufactured item. If applicable, the quality control manager defines the item's testing requirements and the policies for batch and/or serial tracking.

Approve a new item for sales, purchasing and inventory You can define restrictions (aka stopped flags) about item usage within a company, so that removal of the restrictions represents an item approval step. The restrictions consist of three policies to prevent purchase orders, prevent sales orders and prevent inventory transactions for an item.

3.3 Essential Data for using a New Item Within AX

The typical process to define a material item involves many different fields and policies, and different roles have responsibility for this data. However, several company-level policies represent the absolute minimum information in order to use a new item within AX. These policies are termed *essential* item data. The essential data are listed in Figure 3.2 and described below. Two of the policies can be mandated by enterprise-level policies, and two policies only apply to a WMS-enabled item. You can optionally perform a "validation" to determine whether these policies have been specified for an item, and a message displays whether any essential item data is missing.

- *Storage Dimension Group for an Item.* The Storage Dimension Group assigned to an item consists of several policies which can be broadly segmented into two groups. One group of policies involves considerations about site, warehouse and bin locations, and a second group is related to the basic versus advanced approach to warehouse management. Most scenarios only require a few user-defined Storage Dimension Groups. A subsequent section provides further explanation of the Storage Dimension Group policies (Section 3.4).

  When assigned to an item at the enterprise level in a multicompany scenario, the Storage Dimension Group represents a global policy that will be inherited and mandated for the item at all applicable companies. Otherwise, a blank value means each company can assign their own Storage Dimension Group to the item. The most common approach employs a blank value at the enterprise level.

Figure 3.2 Essential Data for using a New Item

Type of Item Information		Level of Information		
		Enterprise	Company	
Item Identifier		Specify Product Number ⇨	Inherit Item Number	
Product Name		Specify Product Name	N/A	
Storage Dimension Group for an Item		Specify as an Enterprise Policy ⇨ or Leave Blank ⇨	Inherit the Enterprise Policy or Assign the relevant Dimension Group to Item	Essential information for using a new item within AX
Tracking Dimension Group for an Item				
Item Model Group		N/A	Assign an Item Model Group to Item	
Item Group			Assign an Item Group to Item	
For WMS-Enabled Item	Reservation Hierarchy		Assign a Reservation Hierarchy to Item	
	Unit Sequence Group		Assign a Unit Sequence Group to Item	

Legend: ⇨ = Release product to a company when using a multicompany approach to item definition

- *Tracking Dimension Group for an Item.* The policies within a Tracking Dimension Group identify the need for tracking batch numbers or serial numbers (or both) for an item. Most multicompany scenarios will assign it to an item at the enterprise level so that it is mandated for all applicable companies. In any case, each company can have a different basis for the assignment of batch numbers or serial numbers. A subsequent section provides further explanation of the Tracking Dimension Group (Section 3.5).

- *Item Model Group.* The Item Model Group assigned to an item consists of multiple policies with a wide variety of impacts. The key policies for a material item include identifying the item as a stocked product and the assignment of an inventory valuation method. The valuation method determines whether actual costing or standard costing applies to an item, and a subsequent chapter provides further explanation of product costing for supporting standard or actual costs (Chapter 4).

  Given the wide variety of policies within an Item Model group, it is easier to provide further explanation within the relevant context. For example, the policy about enforcing approved vendors for a purchased item will be further explained in the context of purchase order processing and approved vendors (Section 8.3). Most scenarios only require a few user-defined Item Model Groups because of similarities in the applicable policies for different groups of material items.

- *Item Group.* The applicable G/L accounts are embedded in the Item Group assigned to the item. Additional G/L accounts related to standard cost items must be specified as part of a posting profile, where the account number assignment may reflect an Item Group or Cost Group or both.

- *Reservation Hierarchy.* A Reservation Hierarchy only applies to a WMS-enabled item, and it indicates how to handle reservation logic at WMS-enabled warehouses. More than one user-defined Reservation Hierarchy may be needed to support the differing reservation logic for normal items versus serialized or batch-controlled items.

- *Unit Sequence Group.* A Unit Sequence Group only applies to a WMS-enabled item, and indicates how to handle an item's UM for warehouse management transactions at WMS-enabled warehouses. For example, an item may have three different units of measure (such each, carton and pallet) with applicable UM conversion factors, and the three different UM are defined as part of a Unit Sequence group. Alternatively, an item may have just one unit of measure (such as each), but the item still requires a Unit Sequence Group with a single UM value. More than one user-defined Unit Sequence Group may be needed to support the differing UM values for different items. A subsequent section provides further explanation about unit of measure considerations for an item (Section 3.8)

3.4 Significance of the Storage Dimension Group for an Item

A user-defined Storage Dimension Group represents one aspect of the essential information that must be assigned to an item, and it consists of several policies which can be broadly segmented into two groups. One group of policies determines the use of site, warehouse and bin locations, and a second group is related to the basic versus advanced approach to warehouse management.

Policies related to the use of Site, Warehouse and Bin Locations
Most scenarios will track an item's inventory by site, warehouse and bin location, while other scenarios simply require site and warehouse. The related policies can reflect several considerations, such as indicating whether the item's coverage planning policies apply to the site or the site/warehouse, and whether the item's purchase prices (and/or sales prices) will represent companywide or site/warehouse-specific values.

Policies related to the Basic versus Advanced Approach to Warehouse Management The policy "use warehouse management processes" indicates a WMS-enabled item, and automatically results in use of the Inventory Status and license plates. A subsequent chapter provides further explanation about the basic versus advanced approach to warehouse management as well as Inventory Status and license plates (Section 10.1).

3.5 Significance of the Tracking Dimension Group for an Item

A user-defined Tracking Dimension Group represents one aspect of the essential information that must be assigned to an item, and it indicates whether serial numbers or batch numbers apply to the item.

Serialized Items A serialized item is identified by several policies embedded in the Tracking Dimension Group assigned to the item. One policy indicates that each serial number identifies an individual unit.[2] Additional policies determine whether the serial number assignment must be tracked throughout inventory (the *Active* policy), or deferred until the product is actually sold (the *Active in Sales Process* policy). A second set of policies (termed the Serial Number Group) is typically assigned to a serialized item that requires inventory tracking. These policies determine whether the serial numbers are assigned manually or automatically. For automatic assignment, the policies indicate the desired serial number mask and when to assign a serial number. It is typically assigned upon arrival which updates inventory balances.

An additional approach to automatic assignment of serial numbers employs an ad hoc serial number mask, which can be defined as part of the item's receipt transaction for purchase orders or production orders. This approach is typically used when serial numbers have already been assigned to the incoming material, and the serial numbers reflect a pattern. For example, the pattern may reflect the same 10 characters and three unique digits in a numerical sequence, so that you could simply identify the fixed characters and a range of numbers to automatically assign the serial numbers.

The Advanced WMS approach involves an additional consideration, since a serialized item must be assigned an appropriate Reservation Hierarchy that includes the serial number. It is typically placed below the location because it is not relevant for reservation logic.

[2] Serial number tracking traditionally refers to a unique serial number for each unit of inventory. AX also supports a single serial number for multiple units of an item (conceptually similar to batch number tracking), but this explanation focuses on serial numbers for individual units.

Batch-Controlled Items A batch-controlled item is identified by a the Tracking Dimension Group assigned to the item, which must include the batch number.[3] A second set of policies (termed the Batch Number Group) is typically assigned to a batch-controlled item. These policies determine whether the batch numbers are assigned manually or automatically. For automatic assignment, the policies indicate the desired batch number mask and when to assign a batch number. It is typically assigned upon arrival which updates inventory balances.

The Advanced WMS approach involves an additional consideration, since a batch-controlled item must be assigned an appropriate Reservation Hierarchy that includes the batch number. The batch number should be placed above the location when it is relevant for reservation logic, otherwise it can be placed below the location when it is not relevant for reservation logic.

Several additional considerations apply to the inventory of a batch-controlled item. This includes vendor batch information, batch attributes, batch disposition codes about restricted usage, shelf life information (for shelf-life items), batch merges, and batch tracking history. These additional considerations fall outside the scope of this essential guide, and are covered in the complete book.

3.6 Using Templates for Partially Populating Item Information

A template can be used to automatically populate many aspects of the company-level information for an item, thereby simplifying the item definition process.[4] The following guidelines describe the creation and use of an item template.

- *Create template based on a released product.* A template can only be created from a selected item on the Released Products form (in edit mode). The desired template information should be populated for the item prior to creating the template, and the template name should reflect the nature of the information. Most firms will employ several templates that reflect their dominant business models for items. A simplistic example would be a

[3] The term batch number is used because Dynamics AX employs the term lot number as a system-assigned internal identifier for inventory transactions.

[4] Dynamics AX provides two basic approaches to templates which differ in their creation and use. The item template represents the unique approach in terms of how you create it, and how it can be applied after creating an item. All other templates employ a different approach to creation, and they can only be used when you initially create a record (such as a new customer or a new delivery mode). They cannot be applied after you create a record.

template for a material item with batch tracking and an inventory UM of kilograms; another example would be a template for a material item with an inventory UM of each and no batch tracking.

When creating a template, you designate whether it represents a personal template or shared template. Personal templates are only available to the user who created the template, whereas a shared template can be accessed by any user.

- *Applying a template to an already-released product.* Applying a selected template will update the item information for the selected item. The initial step involves selecting the relevant item on the Released Products form, and then applying the template. This approach allows you to release products and then mass update the information for a newly-created item number.

- *Applying a template when creating items via the single-company approach to item definition.* You select the desired template as part of the Create Product dialogue.

Some aspects of item information cannot be updated from a template, since they reflect additional tables that must be populated. For example, this includes lead times and order modifiers (defined on the Default Order Settings form), and item costs for a specified costing version (defined on the Item Price form). Figure 3.3 provides additional examples of item information that can and cannot be populated by item templates.

3.7 Descriptive Information About an Item

Several types of descriptive information can be defined for a product and an item. This includes the enterprise-level information such as the Product Name and Extended Description, as well as company-level information such as physical dimensions.

Product Name and Extended Description The descriptive information for a product number consists of two fields -- for a product name and an optional extended description -- that represent enterprise-level data for an item. The Product Name field is a fixed length field where the number of characters can be easily expanded. The Extended Description field consists of unlimited descriptive text. Language-specific translations can be defined for both fields. The item's extended description is automatically inherited by a sales order line or purchase order line, and it can be optionally overridden.

Figure 3.3 Examples of Item Information Populated by Templates

Category of Information	Populate via Template	Cannot Populate via Template
Engineering	Production Type	
Planning	Coverage Group	
Inventory Management	Inventory UM Storage Dimension Group Tracking Dimension Group Reservation Hierarchy * Unit Sequence Group *	Item-specific UM conversions Physical dimensions of different UM for item Policies for planned transfer orders
Manufacturing		Order quantity modifiers for production Production lead time
Procurement	Company-wide preferred vendor Buyer responsibility Default purchasing UM	Approved vendors for item Vendor item number Purchasing lead time Order quantity modifiers for purchase orders
Sales	Default sales UM Alternative product for sales	Customer item number Order quantity modifiers for sales orders
Accounting	Item Group (G/L account numbers) Financial dimension for item Item Model Group (Std vs Actual Cost)	Standard cost for an item
Quality Management	Batch numbering policy Serial numbering policy	Product testing requirements for an item Batch attributes for an item

Document Handling Capabilities (aka Attachments) The document handling capabilities apply to products and items, and allow entry of extended text using a document type of "Note". Other document types include Word files, Excel spreadsheets, images and various file formats. One or more documents can be attached to a product or an item. These document handling capabilities apply to more than just items; they apply to almost every construct within AX, ranging from master files and setup information to orders and invoices.

A document type of note has several additional characteristics. A note document related to an item number can be inherited by a sales line or purchase line for the item; a note document can also be added manually to the line item. In addition, you can designate whether a note document relates to internal or external purposes. For example, an external note document assigned to a sales line or purchase line can be optionally printed on order documents, as defined by the form setup policies for each type of document. The ability to create types of note documents -- and then assign the note type to a note -- can be creatively used for classification purposes, such as note types related to customer instructions about delivery or material handling. These classifications can then be used to selectively print the type of note document.

The document handling capabilities are also used to support MSDS documents for regulated products, and to support printing of these documents with a sales order packing list or invoice.

3.8 Unit of Measure Considerations for an Item

Considerations about an item's unit of measure (or UM for short) are often important for multiple groups within a company, including purchasing, sales, engineering, production and warehousing. Each group sometimes has unique requirements for an item's UM, The unit of measure codes and the assignment of an item's authorized UM represent enterprise-level information, whereas other UM considerations represent company-level information. These considerations are reflected in the following topics within the section.

- Definition of Unit of Measure Codes
- Inventory UM for an Item
- Authorized UM for an Item
- Weight/Volume and Physical Dimensions for an item's UM
- Default UM for Sales or Purchases of an Item
- UM Considerations for the Advanced WMS approach

Definition of Unit of Measure Codes The unit of measure codes represent enterprise-level information that is language specific. The codes for two different systems of units – metric units and US standard units – are automatically loaded into AX, along with the unit conversion factors (such as grams per kilogram). Additional units of measure must be defined (such as box and case), and the UM conversion factors are often item specific (such as the number of items per box).

Inventory UM for an Item Each item requires one UM for costing and inventory purposes. This is termed the inventory UM or base UM. An item's inventory UM is reflected in its inventory balances, replenishment calculations, product costs, and many of the inventory transactions. It is also reflected in the definition of BOM and routing information for a manufactured item, where component quantities and time requirements are typically expressed per the item's inventory UM. The inventory UM for an item cannot be changed after you report inventory transactions, so the assignment of an inventory UM requires careful consideration.

Authorized UM for an Item The item's inventory UM represents an authorized UM for the item. Any other UM must be authorized before it can be used for the item. An authorized UM means it has a UM conversion factor that ties it back to the item's inventory UM. Standard UM conversions apply to UM codes representing metric or US standard units, such as conversions between kilograms, grams, and milligrams. Additional UM codes such as box and case may need to be defined, along with their UM conversion factors for an item. When entering transactions for an item, you can view an item's authorized UM in the drop-down list for the UM field.

Weight/Volume and Physical Dimensions for an item's UM An item's weight/volume and physical dimensions can be defined via two options. As the preferred option, you define this information for one or more of the item's authorized UM (including the item's inventory UM) using the Physical Dimensions form. The volume is automatically calculated based on the physical dimensions. Alternatively, you can define this information for just the item's inventory UM using the Released Products form. The first option represents a greater level of specificity for the source of information used by the system, and it can automatically populate the fields maintained by the second option. The weight, volume and dimensions have an implied unit of measure (such as pounds, cubic inches and inches), which means that a consistent interpretation should be applied to the values.

Default UM for Sales or Purchases of an Item You can optionally specify an item's default UM for sales orders and purchase orders. These represent companywide defaults for the item with the following impacts.

- *Default UM for Sales Orders.* An item's default sales UM applies to the definition of its order quantity modifiers for sales orders (for a minimum, multiple, maximum, and standard order quantity). The item's default sales UM and order quantity modifiers are normally reflected in a manually entered sales order line. However, when you specify a sales agreement for the sales order, the item's sales UM will default to the sales agreement.

- *Default UM for Purchase Orders.* An item's default purchase UM applies to the definition of its order quantity modifiers for purchase orders (for a minimum, multiple, maximum, and standard order quantity). The item's default purchase UM and order quantity modifiers are normally reflected in a manually entered purchase order line. However, when you specify a purchase agreement for the purchase order, the item's purchase UM will default to the purchase agreement.

Many items only require a single unit of measure. In these cases, you can simplify system usage by assigning the same UM to the item's inventory UM and to the item's default UM for purchase orders and sales orders.

UM Considerations for the Advanced Approach to Warehouse Management The advanced approach employs license plates, where the assignment of a license plate ID often reflects a physical pallet. An item typically has a standard quantity per physical pallet, and you define the associated UM conversion. Some items involve additional UM conversion factors, such as pieces per box and boxes per physical pallet.

These UM considerations must be reflected in the Unit Sequence Group assigned to the item, which defines several warehouse policies related to the use of mobile device transactions -- especially for receipts. You typically define several Unit Sequence Groups reflecting the common UM considerations related to your products, and then assign the applicable group to each item. For example, the group should include a UM code that represents an item's inventory UM and another UM code representing a physical pallet. Several additional policies apply to the UM codes within a Unit Sequence Group. For example, by identifying the UM code that represents a physical pallet for the item (and an item's standard quantity per physical pallet), the system will suggest the number of license plates when receiving a large number of pieces.

3.9 Additional Information for a Purchased Item

A purchased item is typically indicated by its primary source of supply of planned purchase orders (as part of the item's coverage planning data). However, purchase orders can be created for any material item.

The definition of information for a purchased item involves several activities performed by different roles, such as the purchasing agent, cost accountant and quality manager. Various aspects of defining a purchased item are summarized in this section, along with references to more detailed explanations.

- Define and enforce approved vendors for an item (Section 8.3)
- Define purchase prices and discounts for an item using trade agreements (Section 8.4) or blanket purchase orders (Section 8.5)
- Define planning data for a purchased item (Section 5.3)
- Define standard costs for a purchased item (Section 4.1)
- Define serial or batch tracking policies for an item (Section 3.5
- Define batch attributes for a batch-controlled item
- Define testing requirements for an item
- Define a vendor item number (or other alternative identifiers) for an item
- Assign the item to a category hierarchy for procurement purposes

A procurement category hierarchy consists of different nodes that reflect a classification of purchased products, and you assign purchased products to the relevant node (aka the product category). This information can be used in several ways. For example, you can define a purchase agreement and an associated discount percentage based on a total commitment value for a specified product category. The product categories can also be used for purchase spend analysis.

3.10 Additional Information for Manufactured Items

A manufactured item is typically indicated by its primary source of supply of planned production orders (as part of the item's coverage planning data). An additional policy – termed the Production Type – also indicates a manufactured item. A Production Type of BOM enables you to create a bill of material and production orders for the item, whereas a Production Type of None indicates a purchased item and prevents the creation of BOMs and production orders.

The definition of information for a manufactured item involves several activities performed by different roles, such as the product designer, process engineer, production planner, cost accountant and quality manager. Various aspects of defining a manufactured item are summarized in this section, but further explanation falls outside the scope of this essential guide.

- Define the bill of material (BOM) or formula for a manufactured item
- Define the routing for a manufactured item
- Define the BOM and routing for a subcontract manufactured item
- Calculate standard costs for a manufactured item
- Calculate planned costs for a manufactured item
- Define planning data for manufactured item
- Define serial or batch tracking policies for a manufactured item
- Define batch attributes for a batch-controlled item
- Define testing requirements for a manufactured item

With the current AX design, a product must be released to a company before you can define its BOM and routing information as part of the company-level information for the manufactured item.

3.11 Additional Information for a Salable Item

A salable item does not require any special designation, and sales orders can be created for any material item. Several aspects of a salable item are summarized in this section, along with references to more detailed explanations.

- Define sales price trade agreements (Section 7.4)
- Define sales agreements for blanket sales orders (Section 7.5)
- Assign the start dates for selling and shipping a new product
- Manage direct delivery orders for a purchased item (Section 7.3)
- Manage special orders for a purchased item (Section 7.3)
- Manage a production order linked to a sales order
- Define a customer item number (or other alternative identifiers) for an item
- Assign the item to a category hierarchy for sales purposes

A sales category hierarchy consists of different nodes that reflect a classification of salable products, and you assign salable products to the relevant node (aka the product category). Case 3.2 provides an illustration. This information can be used in several ways. For example, you can automatically create sales order lines via selection of products from a sales category hierarchy, or define a sales agreement and an associated discount percentage based on a total commitment value for a specified product category. The product categories can also be used for sales analysis purposes.

3.12 Company versus Site/Warehouse Information for an Item

The concept of company- versus site/warehouse-specific information applies to several aspects of item information. The concept is introduced now and subsequent chapters provide more detailed explanations. Figure 3.4 summarizes some of the major examples of company versus site/warehouse information.

The companywide item information includes the item identifier and inventory UM. Other aspects of an item can reflect companywide information, or site- and warehouse-specific information. For example, an item's companywide information includes the costing method for standard versus actual costing. An item's standard costs can only be maintained as site-specific information, whereas an item's actual costs can be tracked by site or warehouse.

Figure 3.4 Companywide versus Site/Warehouse Information for an Item

<table>
<tr><th colspan="2"></th><th colspan="3">Level of Information</th></tr>
<tr><th colspan="2">Type of Information</th><th>Company-Wide</th><th>Site-Specific</th><th>Warehouse-Specific</th></tr>
<tr><td rowspan="2">Basic</td><td>Item Identifier</td><td rowspan="3">Yes</td><td rowspan="3" colspan="2">N/A</td></tr>
<tr><td>Inventory UM</td></tr>
<tr><td rowspan="3">Costing</td><td>Costing Method (Standard vs Actual)</td></tr>
<tr><td>Standard Cost for Item</td><td rowspan="2">N/A</td><td>Yes</td><td></td></tr>
<tr><td>Actual Cost for Item</td><td colspan="2">Yes</td></tr>
<tr><td rowspan="5">Planning</td><td>Approved Vendor</td><td>Yes</td><td colspan="2">N/A</td></tr>
<tr><td>Primary Source of Supply</td><td rowspan="4">Specify
(Act as default)</td><td rowspan="4" colspan="2">Override
the default</td></tr>
<tr><td>Coverage Group (Set of Policies)</td></tr>
<tr><td>Preferred Vendor</td></tr>
<tr><td>Purchasing Lead Time</td></tr>
<tr><td rowspan="2">Price</td><td>Purchase Price Trade Agreement</td><td rowspan="2" colspan="3">Yes</td></tr>
<tr><td>Sales Price Trade Agreement</td></tr>
<tr><td rowspan="2">Mfg</td><td>BOM for a Manufactured Item</td><td>Yes</td><td>Yes</td><td rowspan="2">N/A</td></tr>
<tr><td>Routing for a Manufactured Item</td><td>N/A</td><td>Yes</td></tr>
</table>

The companywide information for a purchased item includes its approved vendors. It also includes the default values for the item's coverage planning policies -- such as the preferred vendor -- which can be overridden as site/warehouse-specific policies. In addition, the applicability of sales and purchase trade agreement information can be companywide or site/warehouse-specific, as defined by the policies embedded in the Storage Dimension Group assigned to an item.

A manufactured item produced in more than one site can have a companywide BOM that applies to all sites, or it can be site-specific. In contrast, the routing for a manufactured item must be site-specific, and resources must be site-specific.

3.13 Inventory Costing and Financial Reporting for Items

Several item-related policies impact inventory costing and financial reporting for items. These policies include the inventory valuation method, the item group, and the financial dimension assigned to an item, as described below.

Inventory Valuation Method Item costs provide the basis for valuing inventory transactions. An item's costs can be based on a standard costing or actual costing method (such as FIFO, LIFO, and weighted average cost), as defined by the costing method policy embedded in the Item Model Group assigned to the item. Chapter 4 provides further explanation about maintaining standard costs and actual costs.

G/L Accounts and the Item Group The Item Group assigned to an item defines the G/L account numbers impacted by the item's inventory transactions. For example, some of the key G/L accounts include inventory, revenue, cost of goods sold (COGS), and purchase price variances. The item groups and their G/L account numbers do not need to reflect product lines when using a financial dimension for items. For example, the value for the item's financial dimension supports revenue, COGS and inventory by product line.

The item groups assigned to purchased items typically have a parallel with the cost groups assigned to these same items. Cost groups serve a slightly different purpose, since they provide cost group segmentation in the calculated costs of manufactured items. The cost groups also provide an alternative approach for assigning G/L account numbers related to standard cost variances, as illustrated in Case 7.8.

The item groups can serve several other purposes in addition to the assignment of G/L account numbers. For example, they can be used in sales analysis and demand forecasts by item group, or they may represent similarities in the item's production process. These other purposes often result in multiple item groups with the same G/L account numbers.

Financial Dimension assigned to Items The combination of a financial dimension value and G/L account number provide the basis for financial reporting. With a product line dimension, for example, you define the possible values for different product lines. The applicable value for a product line can then be assigned to an item, which will be inherited by any item-related transaction. Financial dimensions can also be assigned to other entities such as customers, vendors, and sites to support multidimensional reporting.

3.14 Workspaces Related to Item Definition

Several predefined workspaces are related to item definition, as described in the following summary of each workspace and its applicable functionality.

Released Product Maintenance Workspace This workspace identifies items with a stopped flag for sales, purchasing and/or inventory. Removal of the stopped flags represents an approval step in the typical process to define a material item (Section 3.2). It also identifies recently released products.

Product Readiness for Discrete Manufacturing Workspace The Product Readiness workspace has two variations -- one for discrete manufacturing (using the BOM approach to product structure) and one for process manufacturing (using the Formula approach). Both variations identify items with incomplete information or an expected change. For example, an expected change can reflect a product change case for an item, or an item's BOM version expiring within the lead time for the manufactured item.

Cost Administration Workspace This workspace identifies items with a missing active cost, including standard cost items without an active item cost record.

Product Variant Model Definition Workspace This workspace summarizes several aspects of information about product masters, including the use of predefined variants as part of item identification.

Category and Product Management Workspace This workspace focuses on the use of product categories, especially for retail purposes. You can view and maintain information about products by category and the released products by category.

3.15 Additional Case Studies

Case 3.1: Enterprise-Level Policies for Items in a Multicompany Supply Chain A manufacturing/distribution business modeled their multicompany operation using multiple companies within an AX instance, and goods flowed between different AX sites/warehouses in the different companies. As part of the enterprise-level policies for items, they standardized their item identification and product names, the UM conversion factors and NMFC code for each item, and enforcement of batch number tracking. Other company-level policies and data about each item were considered to be the responsibility of each company.

Case 3.2: Product Categories for Sales Purposes An equipment manufacturer defined a three level category hierarchy to support sales-related trade promotions. The lowest level of the category hierarchy -- termed the product category -- was assigned to each saleable product. The category hierarchy represents enterprise-level information for an item. Figure 3.5

summarizes an example of the category hierarchy for sales. As noted in the figure's comments, one level in category hierarchy (the brand level) is also mirrored in the business unit financial dimension assigned to an item number, which represents company-level information and supports financial reports by brand.

Figure 3.5 Example Category Hierarchy for Sales Purposes

Level	Description	Examples	Comments
0	Sales Hierarchy	N/A	Brand also defined as a Business Unit Financial Dimension, with a value assigned to an Item Number
1	Brand	SuperTech	
2	Family	Appliances	
3	Product Category	Blenders	
N/A	Product	12345	Product Category assigned to a Product Number

Case 3.3: Variant Codes for Hardware A hardware manufacturer of screws, bolts and nuts was considering the use of variant codes to replace their current item numbering scheme. The current scheme used significant digits in the item number to represent a product, its characteristics, and its pack sizes. For example, the characteristics of a bolt included length, diameter, finish, and head type, and the pack sizes included 10, 100, and 500 counts. The existing item master had thousands of item numbers reflecting different combinations of these attribute values. The number of new items was growing to meet customer-specific demand for additional variations. The proposed scheme consisted of an item number to represent the product (such as a type of bolt) and several variant codes to represent the product characteristics and pack sizes. The proposed scheme would simplify data maintenance about item identification, such as simply adding new values for relevant variant codes and automatically creating new combinations of the values.

Case 3.4: Customer Supplied Material An item representing customer supplied material was used as a component in a manufactured product. The item was treated just like any other purchased material, except that its site-specific standard costs were assigned a zero value. This approach supported BOM information about the component, and also provided visibility of requirements, coordination via purchase orders, and tracking of receipts, inventory and material usage.

Case 3.5: Using Alternative Identifiers in Purchase Order Receiving The incoming material at a manufacturing/distribution company was frequently labeled with the vendor's item number, a UPC code or a special bar code. When reporting purchase order arrival via the mobile device (using advanced warehouse management), the receiving clerk could simply enter any of these alternative identifiers and the system automatically converted it to the internal item number.

Case 3.6: Country of Origin for Purchased Material A company purchased several materials other countries. For a given item, the country of origin was specified as part of the foreign trade information for the item. However, some batch-controlled items were sourced from more than one country. They recorded the country of origin as part of the vendor batch details for each batch of these purchased items. Most cases involved a single country of origin, although a few required two different countries. This information was used to support government reporting requirements about country of origin.

3.16 Executive Summary

Item identification, units of measure, and descriptive information represent some of the basic issues for implementing an ERP system in distribution and manufacturing firms. Item definition involves enterprise- and company-level information, and considerations about companywide versus site/warehouse-specific information. This chapter included a typical business process for defining material items, and summarized the key information of purchased items, manufactured items and salable items. It covered several aspects of inventory costing and financial reporting for items, alternative identifiers for items, and the use of variant codes for item identification purposes. Several case studies illustrated different aspects of item information, such as the use if variant codes, product categories, alternative identifiers, and enterprise-level policies for an item.

Chapter 4

Basics of Product Costing

Product cost information defines the value of an item's inventory transactions. The primary variations in product costing involve standard versus actual costs, and purchased versus manufactured items. For a manufactured item, the calculation of product costs reflects the item's BOM and routing information.

Product cost information represents one of the more complex and critical aspects of an integrated ERP system, especially in manufacturing scenarios. This chapter summarizes several key aspects of product costing, and focuses on purchased material rather than manufactured items. The key aspects include the item cost records within a costing version for standard cost purposes, and the different approaches for actual costing.

1. Summary of Costing Versions
2. Summary of Standard Cost Variances
3. Actual Costing Approaches

4.1 Summary of Costing Versions

A costing version contains the cost records for items, and for labor rates and overhead formulas in manufacturing scenarios. You designate whether a costing version contains standard costs or planned costs. With a version containing standard costs, the cost records about items define their site-specific standard costs. A costing version containing planned costs is used for simulation purposes, such as calculating a manufactured item's planned cost.

Different Costing Versions for Standard Costs The significance of a costing version depends on how you conceptualize your approach for maintaining standard costs. A common approach consists of multiple costing versions that represent standard costs for different calendar years (or quarters).

With this approach, you maintain all item cost records within one costing version that represents the current calendar year, and use an additional costing version for maintaining next year's standard costs. You can copy the active cost records from one costing version to create pending cost records in the other cost version, thereby providing a starting point for updating next year's standard costs. These pending cost records would then be activated at the beginning of the year.

Other approaches reflect a different conceptualization. For example, multiple costing versions can represent site-specific standard costs for different sites, or each costing version can represent incremental changes to standard costs (including the standard costs for new items).

Different Costing Versions for Planned Costs A costing version for planned costs is primarily used for simulation purposes in manufacturing scenarios. For example, you can calculate the planned costs of manufactured items based on different values for labor and overhead rates, and different values for the item cost records for purchased material.

Other than simulation purposes, the concept of item cost records (within a costing version for planned costs) has limited applicability to items with actual costing as an inventory valuation method. Activating this item cost record simply populates an initial value for the item's actual cost, as displayed in the item master.

4.2 Summary of Standard Cost Variances

A standard cost item is identified by an inventory valuation model of "standard cost" within the Item Model Group assigned to the item. Several types of variances can be generated for a standard cost item, such as purchase price variances, cost change variances, and inventory revaluation variances.

Purchase Price Variance An item's site-specific standard cost provides the basis for calculating purchase price variances at the time of purchase order receipt (reflecting the difference with the purchase order price) and invoice entry (reflecting the difference between the purchase order price and invoice price).

Cost Change Variance Transfers between sites will generate a cost change variance when there are differences between an item's site-specific standard costs. The variance is generated at the time of receipt for a transfer order. An item's standard cost at two different sites can be different for several reasons. For example, the item's costs may be higher because of the associated transfer costs to another site, or because of different manufacturing or purchasing costs.

Inventory Revaluation Variance Activating an item's standard cost record will revalue existing inventory if costs change, and generate a cost revaluation variance. This variance can also be created when converting to a standard cost model, since conversion of an item's financial on-hand inventory to standard costs will generate a variance for the value difference.

Production-Related Variances Production-related variances are calculated after ending a production order for a standard cost item. Four types of variances are calculated: lot size variance, production quantity variance, production price variance, and production substitution variance.

4.3 Actual Costing Approaches

Several inventory valuation models for actual costing are supported by Dynamics AX, as summarized in Figure 4.1. Each item must be assigned an Item Model Group which defines the inventory valuation model and related policies. An actual costing method (except for moving average) requires an inventory closing process at month end, which settles issue transactions to receipt transactions based on the inventory valuation model assigned to an item. It creates adjustments to the value of on-hand inventory quantities based on financially updated receipts.

Figure 4.1 Actual Costing Methods

Inventory Model	Impact of Inventory Model on the Inventory Closing Process
Weighted Average	Issues will be settled against a summarized weighted average for the month
Weighted Average Date	Issues will be settled against a summarized weighted average for each day
FIFO	Issues will be settled against the oldest receipts within monthly period
LIFO	Issues will be settled against the newest receipts within monthly period
LIFO Date	Issues will be settled against the newest receipts closest to the issue date
Basic Rules for the above Inventory Models	An item's issues will be valued at a running average cost (as of the transaction date). The running average cost reflects the average of the financially updated transactions; it can optionally include physically updated transactions. The user can optionally link (aka mark) a specific receipt to a specific issue transaction.
Moving Average	None. Inventory close only closes the accounting period..

4.4 Additional Case Studies

Case 4.1: Maintain Standard Costs in Multisite Operations A manufacturing/distribution company had multiple manufacturing sites producing different end-items that were transferred to different distribution sites. In order to maintain the site-specific standard costs, the cost accountant defined multiple costing versions representing the different sites. After calculating the costs of manufactured items at the manufacturing sites, these costs were copied to the costing versions that represented the site-specific costs for the distribution sites.

Case 4.2: Purchase Price Variances based on Cost Group A manufacturer of printed circuit boards defined one item group representing electronic components that was assigned to the relevant purchased items. In addition, the company defined several cost groups for different types of electronic components such as integrated circuit chips and capacitors in order to support cost group segmentation of a manufactured item's calculated costs. These cost groups (rather than the item group) were also used to assign the G/L accounts for purchase price variances.

4.5 Executive Summary

Product cost information supports valuation of an item's inventory transactions using a standard cost or actual cost method. Standard costs for items are maintained in a set of cost data termed a costing version. Manufacturers can also maintain labor rates and overhead formulas in a costing version, and calculate the costs for manufactured items. For item's with an actual costing approach, the costs are not maintained in a costing version, but reflect financially-updated receipt transactions such as invoiced purchase orders and ended production orders.

Chapter 5

Coverage Planning Data to Model SCM Decision Making

Planned orders communicate the need to replenish an item's inventory, and are generated by master scheduling logic based on an item's coverage planning data and related S&OP game plans. The coverage planning data (or planning data for short) represents a model of decision making about coordinating the supply chain. The planning data differs for purchased items, manufactured items and transfers. Much of this planning data can be assigned as a companywide policy for an item, and optionally overridden as a site-specific or site/warehouse-specific policy. The key planning data includes the coverage group assigned to an item. Each user-defined coverage group consists of multiple policies such as the applicable coverage code and use of action messages. These messages work in conjunction with planned orders to coordinate supply chain activities to meet the S&OP game plans.

This chapter focuses on coverage planning data and the next chapter covers S&OP game plans and master scheduling. The chapter also focuses on the planning data for purchased items and transfers, since manufactured items fall outside the scope of this essential guide. The chapter starts with the significance of coverage groups and the options for a coverage code, and then explains the key planning data for purchased items, manufactured items, and transfers. It addresses several topics within the coverage planning data, such as policies about action messages. These considerations are reflected in the following sections within the chapter.

1. Significance of Coverage Groups
2. Options for a Coverage Code
3. Planning Data for Purchased Items

4. Special Cases for Purchased Items
5. Planning Data for Transfers
6. Additional Planning Data for Master Schedule Purposes
7. Maintain Coverage Planning Data for Items
8. Action Messages and Related Policies
9. Messages about Calculated Delays and Related Policies

5.1 Significance of Coverage Groups

A coverage group consists of multiple policies that provide a model of decision making about coordination of an item's supply chain activities. Each coverage group has a user-defined identifier and name, and a typical company will employ different coverage groups to model the differences in decision-making logic. For example, key aspects of decision-making logic involve the generation of planned supply orders to meet demands, and the use of action messages to coordinate supply orders.

As an explanatory approach, the key policies within a coverage group will be segmented into different topics and covered by different sections. Subsequent sections explain the different options for a coverage code (Section 5.2), action messages and related policies (Section 5.8), and messages about calculated delays and related policies (Section 5.9).

As already noted, a typical company will employ different coverage groups to model the differences in decision-making logic. Case 5.1 illustrates a company that started with just a few coverage groups, and then evolved into more coverage groups.

5.2 Options for a Coverage Code

The coverage code represents a key part of the decision-making logic about generating planned supply orders for an item. It is embedded within the coverage group assigned to an item, but its importance merits a separate explanation. The term coverage code has several synonyms and different ERP systems employ different terms and provide different options. Examples of different terms include the reorder policy and the replenishment policy.

The four options for a coverage code include period (aka period lot-sizing logic), requirement, min-max and manual. The most commonly used options include period and requirement. Each option can be characterized by its primary planning data, order quantity modifiers, and a safety stock approach. These options are summarized in Figure 5.1 and described below. The left-hand columns characterize each option in terms of its underlying logic, such as order point or period lot-sizing logic.

Figure 5.1 Options for a Coverage Code

		Planning Data		
Logic Basis	Coverage Code and its significance	Primary Planning Data	Order Qty Modifiers**	Safety Stock Approach
Period Lot Size	Period Suggested order quantity covers multiple demands within the period subject to order quantity modifiers	Period Size (in days)	Minimum Multiple Maximum	Minimum Quantity*
Order Driven	Requirement Suggested order quantity covers one demand subject to order quantity modifiers		Minimum Multiple Maximum	Minimum Quantity*
Order Point	Min-Max Suggested order quantity achieves maximum inventory quantity subject to order quantity multiple	Minimum Quantity* Maximum Quantity	Multiple	N/A
Manual Planning	Manual No suggested orders	N/A	N/A	N/A

* = The minimum quantity represents a site/warehouse-specific safety stock quantity, and differs from the order quantity modifiers for a minimum.

** = Three different sets of order quantity modifiers can be defined for an item: for sales orders, purchase orders and for production/batch orders. Planned transfer orders use the order quantity modifiers related to production/batch orders.

Period (also known as Period Lot Size) When an item's projected inventory reaches zero (or its minimum quantity), master scheduling logic will suggest a planned order with a quantity that covers demands over the period size, subject to order quantity modifiers. The period size reflects the frequency of replenishment (such as daily, weekly or monthly) and different coverage codes must be defined for each period size. Examples of the user-defined values for a coverage code include *Period-1Day*, *Period-7Days* and *Period-30Days*, where the associated period size reflects the frequency of daily, weekly and monthly replenishment.

The item's minimum quantity for a given site/warehouse represents an explicit inventory plan or safety stock. An implied inventory plan reflects the extent to which the order quantity modifiers (for minimum and multiple) inflate the suggested order quantity so that it exceeds the requirements.

Requirement (also known as Order-Driven or Lot-for-Lot) When an item's projected inventory reaches zero (or its minimum quantity), master scheduling logic will suggest a planned order and quantity that covers each individual demand, subject to order quantity modifiers. As noted above, the minimum quantity and the order quantity modifiers represent explicit and implied inventory plans respectively.

Min-Max When an item's projected inventory falls below its minimum quantity, master scheduling logic will suggest a planned order with a quantity that achieves the item's maximum quantity, subject to an order quantity modifier for a multiple. The projected inventory reflects future demands and scheduled receipts for the item. The values for minimum and maximum quantity are typically specified using a fixed approach, but a variable approach can be used. The fixed approach consists of a single value for each quantity, whereas the variable approach employs a pattern for each quantity such as different quantities for each month to reflect seasonality or trends. Each pattern is termed a minimum/maximum key.

Manual Master scheduling logic will not suggest planned orders, but it does calculate requirements to support manual planning efforts.

Assignment of the Coverage Code to an Item The coverage code is embedded within the coverage group assigned to an item. You assign the coverage group as part of the item master information, but it can be overridden as part of the site/warehouse information for an item. Alternatively, you can just override the coverage code (rather than the coverage group) as part of the site/warehouse information for an item.

Order Quantity Modifiers Three different sets of order quantity modifiers can be defined for an item -- for sales orders, purchase orders and production/batch orders. Planned transfer orders use the order quantity modifiers related to production/batch orders. These order quantity modifiers involve several considerations for planned supply orders.

- *Minimum.* The minimum represents the smallest suggested order quantity.
- *Multiple.* The suggested order quantity will always reflect the multiple, even if it exceeds the maximum.
- *Maximum.* The maximum represents the largest order quantity, so that master scheduling logic will generate multiple planned orders to cover requirements exceeding the maximum.

Some situations require a fixed order quantity, perhaps reflecting considerations about batch tracking, transportation, production or some other factor. In these situations, use the same values for minimum, maximum and multiple so that master scheduling logic will generate multiple planned orders for the fixed quantity.

5.3 Planning Data for Purchased Items

Master scheduling logic will generate planned purchase orders based on an item's planning data. Figure 5.2 summarizes the planning data for purchased items, and highlights the companywide versus site-specific and site/warehouse policies. The information reflects the book's baseline model, where coverage planning applies to the combination of site and warehouse. The bottom of the figure also highlights the four key forms for maintaining an item's planning data. Further explanation covers each aspect of planning data within the figure.

Figure 5.2 Key Planning Data for Purchased Items

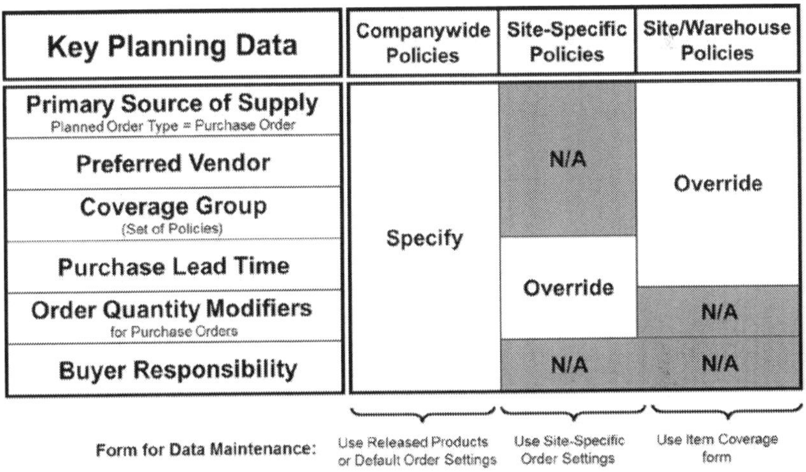

Key Planning Data	Companywide Policies	Site-Specific Policies	Site/Warehouse Policies
Primary Source of Supply (Planned Order Type = Purchase Order)	Specify	N/A	Override
Preferred Vendor	Specify	N/A	Override
Coverage Group (Set of Policies)	Specify	N/A	Override
Purchase Lead Time	Specify	Override	Override
Order Quantity Modifiers for Purchase Orders	Specify	Override	N/A
Buyer Responsibility	Specify	N/A	N/A
Form for Data Maintenance:	Use Released Products or Default Order Settings	Use Site-Specific Order Settings	Use Item Coverage form

Primary Source of Supply A planned order type of Purchase Order indicates the primary source of supply for an item, so that master scheduling logic will generate planned purchase orders. An item's planned order type (aka default order type) can be specified as a companywide policy, and optionally overridden for a given site/warehouse. For example, a purchased item may be replenished via purchase orders at one warehouse, but replenished via transfer orders at a different warehouse.

Preferred Vendor An item's preferred vendor can be specified as a companywide policy, and optionally overridden for a given site/warehouse. It must reflect one of the item's approved vendors when enforcing the policy for approved vendors. Master scheduling logic assigns the preferred vendor to planned purchase orders for the item.

The approach to defining an item's preferred vendor differs slightly for buy-to-order components, or when sourcing to the vendor with the lowest price or delivery lead time. The next section provides further explanation of these special cases for purchased items.

Coverage Group The coverage group consists of multiple policies that provide a model of the decision-making logic about coordination of an item's supply chain activities, as described in the previous section. The companywide policy for an item's coverage group can be overridden for a given site/warehouse. As an alternative approach for overriding the coverage group, you can override selected policies such as the coverage code and period lot size.

Purchase Lead Time An item's purchase lead time can be specified as a companywide policy, and optionally overridden as a site-specific or site/warehouse-specific policy. It is expressed in terms of calendar days unless explicitly flagged as working days. This lead time typically represents the average number of days to receive material after placing a purchase order. It will be used by master scheduling logic to suggest an order date for planned purchase orders. It is also used when manually creating a purchase order to initially calculate the delivery date for the item.

An item's purchase lead time can be optionally specified in purchase trade agreements. However, this information only applies to several special cases described in the next section.

Order Quantity Modifiers for Purchasing The order quantity modifiers consist of a minimum, maximum and multiple. They are expressed in the item's default purchase UM (if specified) otherwise they reflect the item's inventory UM. The order quantity modifiers impact planned purchase order quantities. They are also considered when manually creating or maintaining a purchase order for the item, where a soft warning will be displayed when you enter a quantity that does not meet these criteria. The item's standard purchase order quantity also reflects considerations about these order quantity modifiers, and it acts as a default value when manually entering a purchase order line for the item.

Buyer Responsibility The concept of buyer responsibility provides an organizing focus for communicating the need to synchronize supplies with demands. The concept of buyer responsibility is typically based on the buyer group field; an alternative basis could be the item group field. A user-defined buyer group can be assigned to an item to indicate responsibility for maintaining planning data, whereas the buyer group assigned to a vendor indicates responsibility for coordinating purchases. Master scheduling logic generates planned orders identified with the buyer group associated with the vendor. A purchase order header contains a buyer group that applies to all purchase order line items.

5.4 Special Cases for Purchased Items

The previous section focused on the key planning data for purchased items, and several special cases involve additional considerations. These special cases include purchase lead times within purchase price trade agreements, the suggested vendor for planned purchase orders based on lowest price or delivery lead time, and the use of default ship-to locations.

Purchase Lead Times within Purchase Price Trade Agreements An item's purchase lead time can be optionally specified within the entry for a purchase price trade agreement, such as specifying a longer lead time for a lower purchase price. However, you must explicitly designate usage of this lead time information as part of the entry. When explicitly designated for use, the lead time will be inherited by a manually entered purchase order line that meets the criteria for the trade agreement entry. It will also be inherited by the planned purchase order.

Suggested Vendor based on Lowest Price or Delivery Lead Time Some scenarios will source a purchased item based on price or delivery considerations rather than a preferred vendor. In this case, the preferred vendor field should be left blank in order to support automatic vendor assignment on planned purchase orders based on trade agreement information for lowest price or delivery lead time.[1] The previous point explained the additional consideration for using the purchase lead time associated with trade agreement entry. A subsequent chapter provides further explanation about purchase trade agreements (Section 8.4).

Default Ship-To Location You can optionally specify a default ship-to location for a purchased item (consisting of a specified site or a specified site/warehouse), and even mandate use of the ship-to location. This approach typically reflects a scenario where the purchased item is only used at the specified location. Alternatively, the default ship-to location can be assigned to a vendor.

[1] A companywide policy (defined in the Master Planning Parameters form) determines whether master scheduling logic can use the purchase price trade agreement information to suggest a vendor for purchased items (when a preferred vendor has not been specified). A related policy specifies whether price or delivery lead time serves as the basis for suggesting a vendor.

5.5 Planning Data for Transfers

Master scheduling logic will generate planned transfer orders based on an item's planning data. Figure 5.3 summarizes the key planning data for transfers of an item, and highlights the companywide versus site-specific and site/warehouse policies. The information reflects the book's baseline model, where coverage planning applies to the combination of site and warehouse. The bottom of the figure also highlights the four key forms for maintaining an item's planning data. Further explanation covers each aspect of planning data within the figure.

Figure 5.3 Key Planning Data for Transfers

<table>
<tr><th>Key Planning Data</th><th>Companywide Policies</th><th>Site-Specific Policies</th><th>Site/Warehouse Policies</th></tr>
<tr><td>Primary Source of Supply
Planned Order Type = Transfer</td><td rowspan="2">N/A</td><td rowspan="4">N/A</td><td rowspan="2">Specify</td></tr>
<tr><td>Refilling Warehouse</td></tr>
<tr><td>Coverage Group
(Set of Policies)</td><td>Specify</td><td rowspan="2">Override</td></tr>
<tr><td>Transfer Lead Time</td><td>Specify transport time between warehouse pairs</td></tr>
<tr><td>Order Quantity Modifiers
for Transfer Orders</td><td rowspan="2">Specify</td><td>Override</td><td>N/A</td></tr>
<tr><td>Planner Responsibility</td><td>N/A</td><td>N/A</td></tr>
<tr><td>Form for Data Maintenance:</td><td>Use Released Products or Default Order Settings</td><td>Use Site-Specific Order Settings</td><td>Use Item Coverage form</td></tr>
</table>

Primary Source of Supply Replenishment based on transfers must be designated in the item's site/warehouse-specific coverage data, where you indicate a planned order type of *transfer* so that master scheduling logic will generate planned transfer orders. A related field defines the preferred refilling warehouse.

Refilling Warehouse The preferred refilling warehouse can be defined for transferring individual items to a warehouse (as part of each item's site/warehouse-specific coverage planning policies). Alternatively, it can be defined for an entire warehouse, which indicates that all warehouse inventory will be replenished from one refilling warehouse unless specifically overridden for an individual item.

Coverage Group The coverage group consists of multiple policies that provide a model of the decision-making logic about coordination of an item's supply chain activities, as described in the previous section. The companywide policy for an item's coverage group can be overridden for a given site/warehouse. As an alternative approach for overriding the coverage group, you can override selected policies such as the coverage code and period lot size.

Transfer Lead Time The transfer lead time (aka transportation time or transport days) is expressed in calendar days. It can reflect a warehouse viewpoint or an item viewpoint. With a warehouse viewpoint, you specify the transport days between a pair of warehouses on the Transport form. It reflects a companywide policy for all transfers between the warehouse pair. The item viewpoint supports an item-specific transfer time for handling unusual situations, and is defined as part of the item's site/warehouse-specific coverage planning policies. Most scenarios simply use the warehouse viewpoint.

Order Quantity Modifiers for Transfer Orders The order quantity modifiers consist of a minimum, maximum and multiple. They are expressed in the item's inventory UM. The order quantity modifiers impact planned transfer order quantities. They are also considered when manually creating or maintaining a transfer order line for the item, where a soft warning will be displayed when you enter a quantity that does not meet these criteria. The item's standard order quantity also reflects considerations about these order quantity modifiers, and it acts as a default value when manually entering a transfer order line for the item.

Planner Responsibility The concept of planner responsibility for transfer orders is often based on the ship-from or ship-to warehouse, or the buyer group assigned to the item. For example, master scheduling logic generates planned transfer orders identified with the buyer group and the ship-from/ship-to warehouses, so that a planner can selectively view planned orders for which they have responsibility.

Special Cases for Transfers Some scenarios have adjacent warehouses where planned transfer orders between the warehouses are used to communicate requirements, but without the need for tracking in-transit inventory. Actual transfers between warehouses can be handled through a transfer journal rather than a transfer order. In this case, planned transfer orders can be used to communicate requirements, but firming the planned orders should generate a transfer journal which can be subsequently posted after physically moving the material. This approach requires a site-specific policy termed "Use transfer journals for movements within site" otherwise firming a planned order results in a transfer order.

An alternative solution approach to this scenario involves a one-step transaction for reporting shipment of a transfer order with automatic receipt at the ship-to warehouse.

5.6 Additional Planning Data for Master Schedule Purposes

For master schedule purposes, an additional aspect of planning data involves forecast consumption logic, as defined by several policies within the Coverage Group assigned to these items. Another aspect involves the delivery date control policy assigned to salable items, such as ATP or CTP logic. The next chapter provides further explanation about forecast consumption (Section 6.3) and the delivery date control policy for sales orders (Section 6.5).

5.7 Maintain Coverage Planning Data for Items

The coverage planning data for an item is spread across multiple forms. These include the Released Product Details form for the selected item and the associated form for Default Order Settings. This information represents companywide policies, and the coverage planning data on the Released Product Details form can be populated via a template. The information on two other forms – termed the Site-Specific Order-Settings and the Item Coverage form -- represent site-specific and site/warehouse-specific policies respectively. As a general guideline, you maintain the coverage planning data at the highest possible level unless warranted; this approach reduces the level of data maintenance.

Information on the Item Coverage form can be maintained directly, or you can use a mass maintenance approach using the Item Coverage Setup form. Use of the Item Coverage Setup form provides several advantages.

- View items without any item coverage records, thereby making initial data maintenance easier.
- View a subset of items by filtering on the item group or buyer group, or the currently assigned coverage group or storage dimension group.
- Use the default settings (of a selected record of one item's coverage data) as the copy basis for initially creating a new record for selected items without data.
- Delete the item coverage data records for selected items, so that you have a fresh start at maintaining the data.

5.8 Action Messages and Related Policies

Action messages represent one of the key tools for coordinating supply chain activities to meet the S&OP game plans. However, many companies struggle with effective use of action messages because the volume can easily overwhelm the planner so that the messages become meaningless. This section summarizes the action messages and provides some guidelines for effective usage.

Several action message policies are embedded within the coverage group assigned to an item, and master scheduling logic can generate action messages for planned and actual supply orders. The various types of action messages and related policies are summarized in Figure 5.4. The figure includes information for messages about calculated delays will be covered in the next section.

Figure 5.4 Significance of Action Messages

Type of Message	Significance of Message	Message Filters		
		Suppress	Tolerance	Horizon
Advance (Action Messages)	Expedite the order to an earlier date	Yes/No	Advance Tolerance (in days)	
Postpone (Action Messages)	De-expedite the order to a later date	Yes/No	Postpone Tolerance (in days)	
Increase (Action Messages)	Increase order to a suggested quantity	Yes/No		Look-Ahead Horizon (in days)
Decrease (or Cancel) (Action Messages)	Decrease order to a suggested quantity Cancel order	Yes/No*	N/A	
Derived Actions Policy (Action Messages)	Transfer the action message related to a production order to its component items	Yes/No		
Delay	Projected completion date does not meet requirement date	Yes/No	N/A	Look-Ahead Horizon (in days)

* = Suppressing the decrease message will also suppress the cancel message.

Summary of Action Messages An action message indicates a suggestion to advance/postpone an order's delivery date, to increase/decrease an order quantity, or to cancel a supply order. Message filters can eliminate unnecessary action messages, such as a look-ahead horizon to limit the number of messages and tolerances for the advance and postpone messages. The look-ahead horizon can be specified within a coverage group, or as one of the policies for a set of master plan data.

In many cases, the "advance" action message reflects the rescheduling assumption about an item, where it is generally easier to reschedule an existing supply order than create a new one. That is, master scheduling logic will generate an advance message for an existing order rather than generating a new planned order to cover a requirement that occurs within a relevant time horizon (such as the item's lead time).

Analyzing Action Messages Action messages can be viewed from several different forms for a specified set of master plan data. For example, you can view the action messages for a single item on the Net Requirements form or for all items on the Actions form. The Actions form enables you to apply the suggested action for a selected message, where the applied action depends on the message and the type of supply order, and whether it represents a planned or actual supply order. An associated Apply Action dialogue enables you to specify an additional-but-related impact. For example, when applying a cancel message for a purchase order line (which will delete the line), you can choose to delete the entire purchase order if it was the last line on the order.

From the Actions form, you can also access the Action Graph form to view a graphic analysis of related action messages for a selected message. The related action messages are displayed in a multi-level format when the selected item reflects any part of a supply chain involving production orders and/or transfer orders. In this way, you can analyze the action message for the top-level item that impacts lower level items. You can also apply a suggested action as described above.

Guidelines for Effective Use of Action Messages Many companies struggle with effective use of action messages, often because of the sheer volume of messages and the resulting difficulties in taking action. To really be effective, you should consider ways to reduce the number of messages so that you achieve a target "hit rate" of more than 90% for taking action on the messages.

As a starting point, you can reduce the number of messages by reducing the look-ahead window for each type of message, and/or by adjusting the message filters for advance/postpone messages. One guideline involves minimizing the degree to which you create actual supply orders for future periods (in advance of the order date), since this results in additional messages when demands change. In contrast, the use of planned orders will automatically adjust to demand changes. A high volume of messages often stems from poor S&OP game plans and unrealistic promise dates on sales orders.

5.9 Messages about Calculated Delays and Related Policies

Messages about a calculated delay represent one of the tools for coordinating supply chain activities to meet the S&OP game plans. The messages indicate that the projected completion date for a supply order will cause a delay in meeting a requirement. This is especially relevant for a sales order requirement, but it also applies to a requirement stemming from a demand forecast and/or safety stock. A related supply order typically has an associated "advance" action message. However, the messages about calculated delays also represent one of the more complex aspects of master scheduling logic, and they are suppressed in many scenarios. This section summarizes the messages about calculated delays and provides some guidelines for effective usage.

Summary of Messages about Calculated Delays The policy about using calculated delay messages is embedded within the coverage group assigned to an item, and master scheduling logic can generate messages for planned and actual supply orders. As summarized in Figure 5.4, you can specify a look-ahead window to limit the number of messages or simply suppress them. The look-ahead horizon can also be specified as one of the policies for a set of master plan data, which acts as an override to the value within a coverage group.

Analyzing Messages The messages about calculated delays can be viewed from several different forms for a specified set of master plan data. For example, you can view the messages for a single item on the Net Requirements form.

Guidelines for Effective Use of Messages Many companies struggle with effective use of messages about calculated delays, often because of the sheer volume of messages or because of the complexities associated with using the delayed dates as the basis for requirement dates. As a starting point, you can reduce the number of messages by reducing the look-ahead window. A high volume of messages often stems from poor S&OP game plans and unrealistic promise dates on sales orders.

5.10 Additional Case Studies

Case 5.1: Different Coverage Groups to Model SCM Decision Making

A manufacturing/distribution company employed several different coverage groups within AX to model the SCM decision making of different roles, such as production planners, buyers and DRP coordinators for transfer orders. As a starting point, they defined several coverage groups to reflect the different values for a coverage code, which included the different period lot sizes (such as daily, weekly, bi-monthly and monthly) and the use of min-max logic for generating planned orders. Additional coverage groups were needed for several purposes. First, the master scheduler employed additional coverage groups to support differences in forecast consumption logic. Second, buyers and DRP coordinators employed different groups to support differences in filtering of action message policies, thereby improving the usefulness of action messages. Third, additional groups were needed to identify different safety margins when an item required significant time for picking/shipping or receiving/inspection activities.

Case 5.2 Measuring Improvements in the Models of SCM Decision Making A manufacturing/distribution company was using Dynamics AX to coordinate their supply chain activities. They wanted to improve the effectiveness of system usage based on macro-level quality metrics and periodic sampling. They identified several usage characteristics as the basis for the macro-level metrics, and performed sampling on a weekly basis to measure improvements. Examples of the usage characteristics for different roles such as buyers and DRP coordinators included (1) the percentage of planned orders that reflected the actual SCM decision making, (2) the number of action messages and the percentage that were actually useful, and (3) the number of supply orders and sales order lines with unrealistic or past due dates. These metrics indicated the actual usefulness of the formal system to support SCM decisions, and helped guide incremental efforts to improve system usage.

Case 5.3: Suggested Vendor based on Lowest Price A distributor purchased several items from the vendor offering the lowest price, whereas other purchased items were always sourced from a single preferred vendor. Each vendor provided price quotes for selected items (with date effectivities), and the quotes were used to update purchase price trade agreement information. Using this information, master scheduling logic generated planned purchase orders for the selected items, where the suggested vendor reflected the one with the lowest price.

5.11 Executive Summary

Planned orders communicate the need to replenish an item's inventory, and are generated by master scheduling logic based on an item's coverage planning data and related S&OP game plans. An item's preferred source of supply -- defined on a companywide or site/warehouse-specific basis -- determines whether it reflects a purchase, transfer or production order. This chapter summarized the coverage planning data related to generation of planned orders and the use of action messages and messages about calculated delays. It focused on purchased items and transfers, and did not cover manufactured items.

Chapter 6

Overview of S&OP and Master Scheduling

One of the cornerstones for effective supply chain management in a manufacturing or distribution business consists of effective sales and operations planning (S&OP) game plans. They provide the basis for running the business from the top, and build on the models of the organization's supply chain and decision-making logic. The process typically starts with the definition of all demands for the firm's salable items, and results in S&OP game plans that drive supply chain activities to meet those demands. The nature of an S&OP game plan depends on several factors, such as the need to anticipate demand for an item, the item's primary source of supply, and the need for linkage between a sales order and the item's supply order. Demand forecasts are often used to anticipate demand.

The master scheduling logic within AX plays a critical role in the development and use of S&OP game plans. The term "master scheduling logic" has many different synonyms and the term often varies by ERP software package. Equivalent terms include planning calculations, MRP logic and DRP logic. These planning calculations often reflect one of the more complex aspects of supply chain management and ERP systems.

This chapter reviews common S&OP scenarios and explains the typical business processes to maintain S&OP game plans. It covers key elements of an S&OP game plan, including demand forecasts and sales order promise dates. These considerations are reflected in the following sections within the chapter.

1. Common S&OP Scenarios
2. Typical Process to Maintain S&OP Game Plans for Stocked Products
3. Overview of Demand Forecasts
4. Safety Stock Requirements
5. Sales Order Promise Dates and the Delivery Date Control Policy
6. Workspaces related to Master Planning

Master scheduling logic builds on the supply chain model of a manufacturing or distribution business described in previous chapters. This includes the fundamentals of modeling inventory locations, the definition of material items, and the coverage planning data to model SCM decision making. Subsequent chapters cover other aspects of modeling the supply chain, including sales orders and supply orders.

6.1 Common S&OP Scenarios

The nature of an S&OP game plan depends on several factors, such as the need to anticipate demand for an item, the item's primary source of supply, and the need for linkage between a sales order and the item's supply order. When demand needs to be anticipated, for example, min/max quantities or demand forecasts often provide a key element of S&OP game plans for stocked end-items or stocked components. The item's primary source of supply may reflect production orders in traditional manufacturing or kanban orders in lean manufacturing, as well as purchase orders and transfer orders in a distribution operation. The need for linkage becomes important for make-to-order and buy-to-order products in order to provide visibility of the sales order demand and for tracking actual costs of goods sold. A given company typically has several major scenarios where each scenario employs different key elements in the S&OP game plans.

The common S&OP scenarios differ for manufacturing and distribution operations. This section focuses on S&OP for distribution operations to reflect the topics covered in this essential guide, although it also summarizes some of the considerations for manufacturing.[1]

Several common S&OP scenarios are summarized in Figure 6.1 and described below. For each scenario, the figure identifies the key elements of the S&OP game plan and several additional considerations, including the typical basis of sales order delivery promises. The figure identifies an S&OP scenario for stocked products, where key elements in the S&OP game plan typically include demand forecasts or min-max quantities. The next section describes a typical process to maintain the S&OP game plans a stocked product based on demand forecasts.

[1] More extensive explanations about common S&OP scenarios in manufacturing are provided in the complete book for "Supply Chain Management using Microsoft Dynamics AX: 2016 Edition".

Figure 6.1 Common S&OP Scenarios for Distribution

	Scenario	Key Elements of S&OP Game Plan	Additional Considerations	Basis of Delivery Promises
No Link to Sales Order	Stocked Product	Min-Max Quantities	Coverage Code = Min-Max Calculation of minimum quantity	ATP
		Demand Forecast	Coverage Code = Period Forecast consumption by sales orders versus by all demands Using an inventory plan (safety stock)	
	Buy to Actual Demand	Sales Orders	Coverage Code = Period or Requirement	CTP or CTP via Net Change Explosion
Link to SO	Special Order or Direct Delivery Order	Sales Order with link to Purchase Order	Coverage Code = Period or Requirement	

Stocked Product based on Min-Max Quantities The simplest S&OP approach employs min-max logic to carry inventory in anticipation of actual demand, where an item's coverage planning policies define the minimum and maximum quantities by site/warehouse. The minimum quantity represents an implied demand forecast, where the quantity typically reflects the daily usage rate multiplied by the number of days for the item's lead time. With min-max logic, when an item's projected inventory falls below its minimum quantity, master scheduling logic will generate a planned order that achieves the item's maximum quantity (subject to an order quantity multiple). The values for an item's minimum and maximum quantities can be fixed, or specified as a pattern (termed the minimum key and maximum key). You can automatically calculate the minimum quantity based on historical average usage over the item's lead time, as described in a subsequent section about calculating safety stock requirements (Section 6.4). Sales order delivery promises can be based on available-to-promise (ATP) logic.

Stocked Product based on a Demand Forecast Inventory replenishment based on period lot-sizing logic is driven by the combination of demand forecasts and actual sales orders, which typically involves forecast consumption logic.

The demand forecasts are typically entered for a site/warehouse that represents a selling location, so that forecast consumption logic reflects sales orders shipped from the location. Alternatively, in a multi-level distribution network, the demand forecasts can be entered for a site/warehouse that represents a distribution center within the network (with transfers to the selling locations), so that forecast consumption logic reflects any demands (such as transfer order demands or sales orders).

In addition to the demand forecasts, an inventory plan (expressed as safety stock requirements) can be used to anticipate higher-than-expected customer demand, and meet customer service objectives regarding stock outs, partial shipments and delivery lead times. You can automatically calculate the safety stock requirement based on variations in historical usage and the desired customer service level, as described in a subsequent section about calculating safety stock requirements (Section 6.4).

The number of days for period lot-sizing purposes typically reflects the desired frequency of delivery, with more frequent delivery of A items (such as daily or weekly periods) compared to B and C items (such as monthly periods).

The combination of planned and actual supply orders provide the basis for making delivery promises using ATP logic.

Buy to Actual Demand The S&OP game plan consists of actual sales orders where CTP logic provides the basis for making delivery promises. Alternatively, delivery promises can reflect a quoted lead time that represents the item's lead. The master scheduling task generates planned supply orders to meet the sales order demand, where the planned orders reflect the item's planning data (such as coverage codes of period or requirement). This scenario generally implies a pipeline of sales orders with future delivery dates that exceed the item's lead time, or situations in which customers will wait until delivery

Special Order or Direct Delivery Order Some distribution scenarios handle products via special orders or direct delivery orders, as described in the chapter about sales order processing (Section 7.3). The delivery promises typically reflect CTP logic about the item's lead time. Changes to the sales order do not automatically update the associated purchase order, such as changes in quantity or date. However, master scheduling logic will suggest responses to any changes, such as action messages and/or messages about calculated delays.

Common S&OP Scenarios for Manufacturing The S&OP game plans for make-to-stock products similarly employ demand forecasts, min/max quantities and ATP logic. A completely make-to-order product can be produced to actual demand, although many scenarios employ stocked components (based on demand forecasts) to shorten delivery lead times. CTP logic provides the basis for delivery promises. Some make-to-order scenarios require linkage between the sales order and the end-item's production order, and even linkage to the production orders for lower-level components. A product configurator is typically used for a configure-to-order product. Projects are typically used for an engineer-to-order product, where subprojects may be used to model the top levels(s) of the product structure.

6.2 Typical Process to Maintain S&OP Game Plans for a Stocked Product

The S&OP game plans for a stocked product in a distribution operation often involve a combination of demand forecasts and actual sales orders that drive the planned and actual supply orders. These supply orders provide the basis for making delivery promises on sales orders using available-to-promise (ATP) logic.
A typical business process to maintain the S&OP game plan consists of multiple steps performed by different roles, as summarized in Figure 6.2 and described below. In this example, the primary role with responsibility for maintaining the S&OP game plans is identified as an inventory manager or DRP coordinator, but the role title can differ. This role requires an in-depth understanding of sales and supply chain capabilities, as well as the political power to achieve agreed-upon game plans.

Overview The business process starts with the periodic analysis of historical and projected demands in order to prepare a sales plan and inventory plan for each product, where the sales plan is oftentimes expressed in monthly increments. The inventory plan covers higher-than-anticipated sales order demands to meet desired customer service levels. The inventory manager translates this information into entries for the item's demand forecast and safety stock requirements. After the master scheduling task has been performed, the inventory manager analyzes the results to determine the need for adjustments, and to firm (or approve) planned orders. The planned and actual supply orders provide the basis for realistic promised delivery dates using available-to-promise logic, typically in the context of customer service reps entering sales order lines for the item. In this scenario, actual sales orders consume the item's demand forecast within user-defined forecast periods.

For most scenarios, coverage planning applies to the site/warehouse level, and period lot sizing logic applies to the coverage code assigned to stocked products. The period lot size (expressed in days) represents the frequency of replenishment, and the planned order quantities and dates reflect the time increments and due dates for demand forecasts.

Figure 6.2 Typical Process to Maintain S&OP Game Plans for a Stocked Product in a Distribution Operation

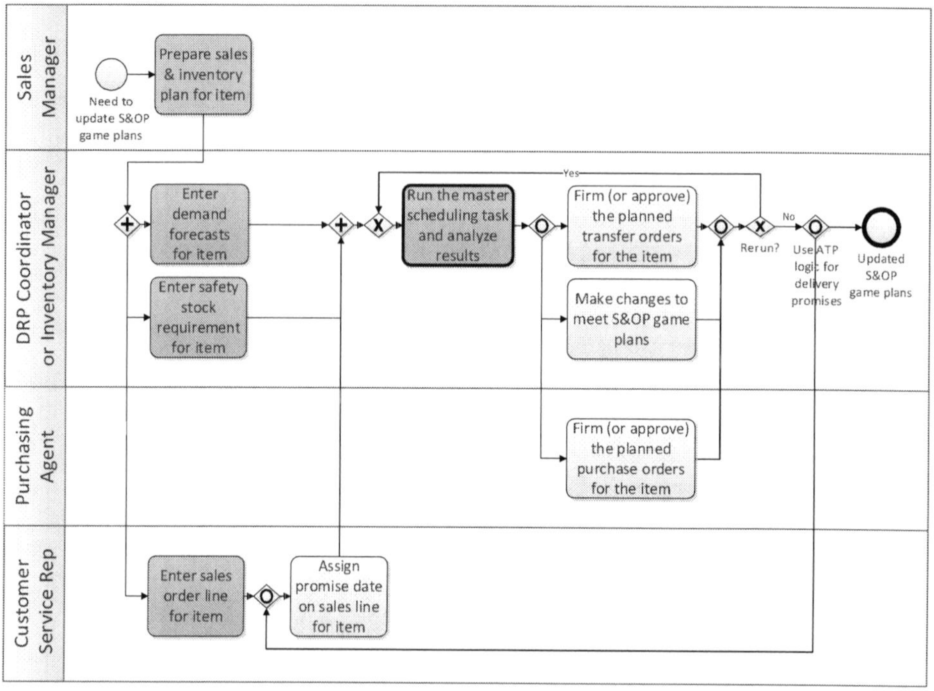

Prepare a sales plan and inventory plan for the item A sales manager role generally has responsibility for analyzing historical and projected demands for the item in order to prepare a sales plan by ship-from location, typically expressed in monthly increments. In many cases the inventory manager must assume this responsibility. The analysis also results in an inventory plan for the item (by ship-from location) to meet the desired customer service levels when actual demands exceed forecast. The analyses may reflect a statistical forecasting technique or some other method.

Enter demand forecast for the item The inventory manager translates the item's sales plan into entries for demand forecasts, typically expressed in weekly increments (or even daily increments) in the near term. In this scenario, actual sales orders for an item will automatically consume the item's demand forecast within the user-defined forecast periods.

Enter safety stock requirement for the item The inventory manager translates the item's inventory plan into entries for a safety stock requirement. The safety stock requirements are typically entered as a single value, although they can also be defined as a pattern of multiple values for different time periods.

Run the master scheduling task and analyze results This activity represents a sub-process with multiple steps and roles. After running the master scheduling task, the inventory manager analyzes the results to identify potential constraints related to material or capacity, and potential problems in meeting demands. The results include planned orders, action messages, and net requirements for material items.

Firm (or approve) the planned transfer orders for the item The inventory manager or a DRP coordinator can firm (or approve) the planned transfer orders between locations, and the suggested quantities and/or dates may be adjusted. By approving a planned order, master scheduling logic will treat the planned order as if it has been scheduled for the specified quantity and due date, and will not delete it. You still need to firm the approved planned order to create an actual supply order,

Firm (or approve) the planned purchase orders for the item A purchasing agent typically firms the planned purchase orders that reflect the S&OP game plans and the model of SCM decision making logic. The suggested quantities and/or dates may be adjusted on planned orders prior to firming.

Make changes to meet the S&OP game plans The DRP coordinator and purchasing agent may need to coordinate several types of changes to meet the S&OP game plans. For example, the changes often involve expediting of existing purchase orders or transfer orders. The changes may also involve working with customer service representatives to delay the promised delivery date on sales orders.

Enter sales order line for item The customer service rep enters sales orders for the item, where each sales line indicates a quantity, ship-from location, and a requested ship date and delivery date. Based on forecast consumption logic, the actual sales orders for an item will automatically consume the item's demand forecast within the forecast period.

Assign promise date on sales line for the item When the customer service rep creates a sales order line for the item, the earliest possible dates for shipment and delivery are automatically assigned based on available-to-promise (ATP) logic. This helps align actual sales orders to the S&OP game plans. The customer service rep can view available to promise information to answer questions about availability, or disable the delivery date control logic to assign an unrealistic promise date. In scenarios where the item is stocked at multiple locations, the customer service rep may evaluate the delivery alternatives for different ship-from locations and then update the sales line based on the selected option.

6.3 Overview of Demand Forecasts

Demand forecasts often represent one of several key elements in the business process to maintain S&OP game plans. However, a comprehensive explanation about the use of demand forecasts falls outside the scope of this essential guide, and is covered in the complete book. This section provides an overview of demand forecasts, starting with the identifier for a set of forecast data and how to enter a demand forecast for an item. It also summarizes the basics of forecast consumption logic, and the options to calculate demand forecasts based on historical data.

Forecast Models and the Identifier for a Set of Forecast Data A set of forecast data has a user-defined identifier termed a forecast model. You specify the forecast model identifier when entering the forecasted quantities and dates for an item. You also specify the relevant forecast model for use in the master scheduling task. Different sets of forecast data can be identified by different forecast model identifiers, but we'll focus on the forecast model containing the current forecast continuously updated as part of the S&OP game plans. A commonly-used identifier for the forecast model is *Current-Forecast* or simply *Forecast*.

Entering a Demand Forecast for an Item Each forecast entry minimally consists of the forecast model, the item identifier, quantity, date, and ship-from site/warehouse. All of the forecast entries with the same forecast model comprise a set of forecast data. Other approaches to entering a demand forecast require additional information, such as forecasts by customer, forecasts for a group of items, and translating monthly or weekly demand forecasts into daily increments.

Basics of Demand Forecast Consumption The combination of demand forecasts and actual demand must be considered to avoid doubled-up requirements for an item. These considerations are commonly termed forecast consumption logic. A basic choice concerns the reduction principle option within the master plan policies for the current master plan, and standard AX supports four major options. This explanation covers the dominant option, where sales orders consume demand forecasts within monthly time buckets.[2]

[2] In AX terminology, this option consists of a reduction principle of *Transactions - Reduction Key,* and the option requires two related policies for an item. One of these policies indicates the applicable reduction key,

This option is easiest to explain using a reduction key comprised of fixed monthly time buckets and weekly increments of demand forecasts, which also represent dominant business practices. In this example, any sales orders with ship dates within a monthly time bucket will consume the item's demand forecasts within the same monthly bucket, starting with the earliest unconsumed forecast and consuming forward. The demand forecasts within a given month can be over-consumed; there is no carry-forward effect to consume forecasts within a future forecast period. Changing the sales order ship date to another month (especially the confirmed ship date) will consume demand forecasts in the relevant month.

Calculate Demand Forecasts based on Historical Data Some scenarios can benefit from the calculation of demand forecasts based on sales history information. Standard AX functionality supports the calculation of statistical forecasts, and the approach differs between the AX 2012 R3 version and the new Dynamics AX.

- *Calculate Demand Forecasts in AX 2012 R3.* This version introduced one approach to the calculation of demand forecasts, where the forecast models in Microsoft SQL Server Analysis Service are used to create predictions. You can review and adjust these calculated forecasts within an Excel spreadsheet, and upload them automatically into the demand forecast tables within AX.

- *Calculate Demand Forecasts in the new Dynamics AX.* Demand forecasts are calculated using the Microsoft Azure Machine Learning cloud service. The service performs best match model selection and offers key performance indicators for calculating forecast accuracy

6.4 Safety Stock Requirements

Safety stock represents a key element in S&OP game plans for those scenarios with stocked products. Within AX, an item's safety stock requirement is defined by the minimum quantity field. You can manually enter a value, or calculate a proposed minimum quantity based on an item's historical usage and its lead time.[3] The significance of the minimum quantity differs between two major approaches for solving S&OP scenarios with stocked items. One approach employs the minimum quantity as part of min-max logic. The second approach

---

which defines the time buckets for forecast reduction purposes. The second "Reduce Forecast By" policy indicates whether sales orders or all types of demands should consume the demand forecasts.

[3] The calculation of a safety stock quantity reflects an item's fixed lead time. The assignment of these lead times was previously described for purchased items (Section 5.3), and transfer items (Section 5.5).

employs the minimum quantity to represent an inventory plan in combination with demand forecasts. The inventory plan covers demand variability to meet the desired customer service level in order to reduce stock outs, partial shipments, and delivery lead times.

Standard AX functionality supports the calculation of a proposed minimum quantity based on an item's historical usage, either for min/max purposes or for inventory plan purposes to cover demand variability. An item's historical usage reflects all issue transactions during a specified time period, including sales order shipments, inventory adjustments and other issue transactions. The calculations also identify the impact of the proposed minimum quantity on inventory value, and the change in inventory value relative to the current minimum quantities. A printed report summarizes the impacts on inventory value for all items included in the calculations.

You perform these calculations using the Item Coverage Journal form and its related form for journal lines (termed the Item Coverage Journal Lines form). These are commonly referred to as the Safety Stock Journal, and the terms Safety Stock Journal and Item Coverage Journal can be used interchangeably.

6.5 Sales Order Promise Dates and the Delivery Date Control Policy

Realistic promise dates for sales order shipments and deliveries can help improve customer satisfaction and supply chain coordination. The initial assignment of the promise dates should align with the item's S&OP game plan, and a sales line with an unrealistic promise date should be highlighted as an exception requiring follow up. After initial assignment, the dates should be changed to reflect changes in the situation, such as changing dates to reflect customer requests or projected delays. Sales orders with unrealistic or past due dates will negatively impact the usefulness of an item's S&OP game plan and the coordination of supply chain activities. The section focuses on promise dates for sales orders. A similar-yet-different set of policies apply to promise dates for transfer orders.

The assignment of promise dates can be supported by a delivery date control policy. The three major options for a delivery date control policy are labeled *ATP, CTP* and *Sales Lead Time*, and the relevant option depends on the scenario and S&OP approach. All three options enforce basic rules to help ensure realistic promise dates. A fourth option (labeled *None*) will disable enforcement of the basic rules, thereby allowing assignment of unrealistic dates. This fourth option is also referred to as disabling delivery date control.

This section assumes familiarity with the sales order dates for shipment and delivery (Section 7.2). It identifies the basic rules enforced by delivery date control, and then summarizes the options for the delivery date control policy.

Basic Rules for Delivery Date Control Several basic rules can be enforced for the shipment and delivery dates on a sales order header and for each line item, but only when you assign one of the three major options for delivery date control. The following basic rules apply when initially entering a sales order header or line item, and also when entering changes such as a different date, quantity, ship-from location or ship-from address.

- *Calendar for the ship-from warehouse.* The calendar assigned to the ship-from warehouse determines the working days when items can be shipped.

- *Calendar for the customer receiving point.* The calendar assigned to the customer (or the applicable customer address) determines the working days when items can be received.

- *Transportation time to customer.* The number of days for transportation time can be specified for the different combinations of the ship-from warehouse, the delivery address characteristics (such as the country, state, county or ZIP code), and the mode of delivery (such as air or truck).

- *Calendar for mode of delivery.* A calendar can be assigned to various modes of delivery for the ship-from warehouse, where the calendar determines the working days when items can be transported. For example, a truck route may only occur on Thursdays.

- *Order entry deadlines for taking sales orders.* The concept of an order entry deadline means that orders received after a specified time are treated as if they were received the next day. You define a set of deadlines for each day within a week (termed an order entry deadline group), and then assign the deadline group to each customer and site.

- *Sales lead time.* A sales lead time can represent the number of days to prepare a stocked item for shipment (such as a value of 0 or 1 day), or it can represent the quoted lead time for a buy-to-order or make-to-order product. It will be automatically reflected in the shipment date when using any of the three major options. The number of days for sales lead time is specified as a companywide value, and it can be defined as item-specific overrides.[4]

---

[4] As an alternative approach, the number of days for sales lead time can be defined within sales trade agreements, so that an applicable sales line (for the customer and item) inherits the sales lead time as well as the sales price or discount.

Delivery Date Control Options for a Sales Order Line A delivery date control option applies to each sales line, and it is initially inherited from the option assigned to the item. The four options are summarized in Figure 6.3 along the typical scenario. For example, the option for ATP (Available To Promise) is typically assigned to a stocked item, whereas the option for CTP (Capable To Promise) is typically assigned to a buy-to-order or make-to-order item.

Figure 6.3 Delivery Date Control Options for a Sales Order Line

Delivery Date Control Option	Scenario	Comments
Sales Lead Time	Use Basic Rules or Quoted Lead Time	Enforce basic rules for assignment of dates
ATP	Stocked End-Item	Enforce basic rules and use ATP logic for dates Analyze supplies using ATP form
CTP	Make-to-Order or Buy-to-Order End-Item	Enforce basic rules and use ATP logic for dates
None	Allow assignment of unrealistic dates	Ignore basic rules for assignment of dates

- *Using the Sales Lead Time Option.* This option enforces the basic rules for the assignment of dates. In some scenarios, the number of days for "sales lead time" can represent a quoted lead time for the item.

- *Using the ATP Option.* This option typically applies to stocked items, where ATP logic focuses on just the salable item. It enforces the basic rules and employs ATP logic for assignment of dates. The ATP option requires several additional policies about underlying assumptions in order to correctly calculate an available-to-promise date. You can analyze the Available Ship and Receipt Dates form, and optionally transfer a selected set of dates to change either the requested dates or the confirmed dates for the sales line.

- *Using the CTP Option.* This option typically applies to a make-to-order or buy-to-order item. It enforces the basic rules and employs CTP logic for assignment of dates. The CTP option considers available inventory and receipts for the salable item (if applicable), and automatically results in a net change explosion when needed.

- *Using the None Option.* Assigning an option of *none* will disable the rules for delivery date control, thereby allowing assignment of unrealistic dates. As a general guideline, any sales line with this option should be highlighted as an exception or alert requiring follow up.

As an alternative approach, you can initiate a net change explosion for a sales line for calculating a ship date, and it only works when the item's coverage code is other than Manual. You can optionally transfer the calculated date to the confirmed ship date.

Continuous Checking of Sales Order Promise Dates The concept of continuously checking the sales order promise dates is embedded in the messages about a calculated delay generated by the master scheduling task. That is, the message indicates when a sales order ship date cannot be met, and identifies the projected ship date.

6.6 Workspaces Related to Master Planning

The Master Planning workspace summarizes several aspects of information about a selected set of master plan data, including planned orders, action messages, and messages about calculated delays. For example, you can view existing planned orders, analyze an item's requirements profile or supply schedule, and firm (or approve) a planned order.

6.7 Additional Case Studies

Case 6.1: Demand Forecasts for Office Furniture An office furniture distributor stocked different end-items based on demand forecasts, and sales order delivery promises were based on ATP logic. Entries of the demand forecasts reflected weekly increments (with start-of-week due dates) over a rolling three month time horizon and monthly increments for the next nine months. The master scheduler translated the monthly forecasts into the weekly increments and relevant due dates over the rolling three month time horizon. The translation considered months containing 4 versus 5 weeks, and also weeks with less than 5 working days. Forecast consumption logic was based on fixed monthly periods defined by a single reduction key assigned to all items. Sales orders with ship dates in a given month consumed the demand forecasts within the month. As time moved forward, the weekly increments of unconsumed forecast became past-due and were ignored by master scheduling logic.

Case 6.2: Stocked End-Items in a Distribution Network A manufacturing/distribution company had multiple sites consisting of a manufacturing plant, regional distribution centers and selling locations. An end-item's inventory was stocked at a distribution center, and then transferred to a selling location to meet actual sales order demand. In this scenario, they entered the item's demand forecasts for each distribution center, and the transfer order requirements consumed the demand forecasts. This required the correct forecast consumption logic. That is, the coverage group assigned to the item and the warehouse representing a distribution center had a "Reduce Forecast By" policy of "All Transactions" rather just "Sales Orders".

6.8 Executive Summary

The ability to run the company from the top requires a sales and operations planning process that formulates an S&OP game plan for each saleable product. The nature of an S&OP game plan depends on several factors, such as the need to anticipate demand for the item, the item's primary source of supply, and the need for linkage between a sales order and the supply order.

The starting point for each game plan typically involves identifying all sources of demand such as sales orders and forecasts, and forecast consumption logic determines how the combination of these demands will drive supply chain activities. Master scheduling logic helps formulate and analyze S&OP game plans, especially in using multiple sets of data for simulation purposes. Realistic promises for sales order delivery can be based on the S&OP game plans and delivery date control policies that enforce basic rules such as calendars and transport time. Unrealistic promises can be highlighted by disabling the delivery date control logic, and the exceptions should require follow-up.

Chapter 7

Sales Order Processing

Sales orders capture demands for a firm's products and services. They comprise a key element in two larger contexts: the sales and operations (S&OP) game plans driving supply chain activities, and customer service across the customer relationship life cycle. Sales orders may originate from one or more order streams, such as direct customer communication with sales representatives or customer service reps, customer self service via web-based applications, and electronically transmitted customer schedules.

Sales order processing involves a wide spectrum of considerations and many variations in business practices. As an explanatory approach, it is easiest to start with a basic model of sales order processing embedded within AX. The basic model provides a foundation for explaining key considerations and major variations. Examples of major variations include the approach to sales pricing, the use of sales quotations, customer returns and commissions. These considerations are reflected in the following sections within the chapter.

1. Basic Model of Sales Order Processing
2. Key Considerations in Sales Order Processing
3. Major Variations in Sales Order Processing
4. Sales Prices and Trade Agreements
5. Sales Agreements
6. Customer Information
7. Performance Metrics related to Sales Orders
8. Workspaces related to Sales Orders
9. Extended Explanation of Life Cycles related to Sales Order Processing

7.1 Basic Model of Sales Order Processing

The typical steps in sales order processing can vary based on several factors, such as different approaches for creating an order and different approaches for sales order picking/shipping. This section summarizes a basic model of sales order processing. It also identifies the different options for creating a sales order.

Overview of the Basic Model The basic model of sales order processing starts with the role of a customer service rep, and the manual entry of a sales order for standard products. A warehouse worker and shipping clerk perform subsequent steps for sales order picking/shipping, which differ when using the basic versus advanced approach to warehouse management. Both approaches support order-based picking described in the basic model. An accounts receivable clerk completes the process by generating an invoice reflecting actual shipments. These roles and steps are summarized in Figure 7.1 and described below.

Figure 7.1 Basic Model of Sales Order Processing

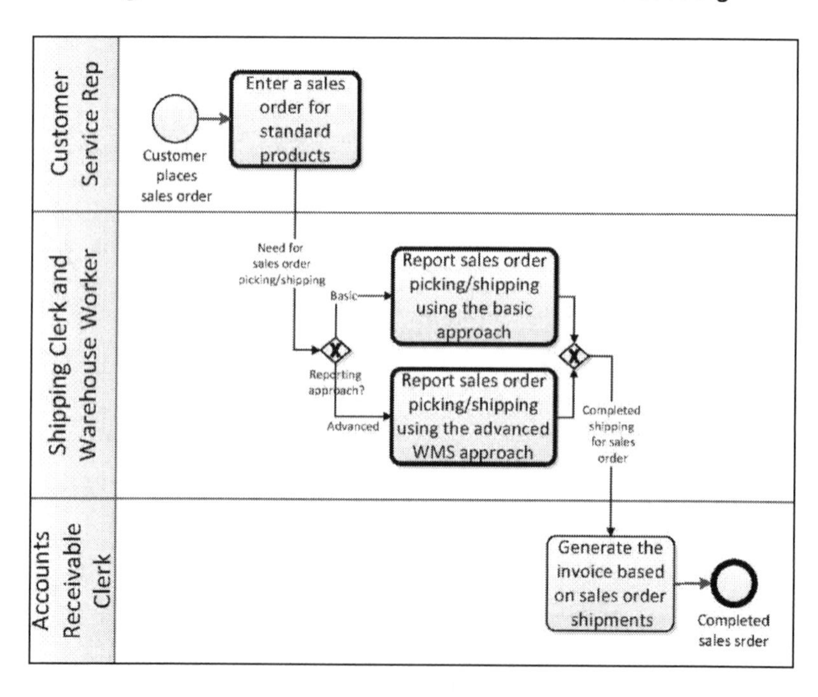

Enter a Sales Order for Standard Products The customer service rep creates a new sales order by starting from the Customer form or the Sales Order form (and using the Create Sales Order dialogue), which results in a sales order header. If needed, the rep maintains aspects of the sales order header information, such as designating (or adding) the desired address or delivery mode, or overriding information inherited from the customer master. The customer service rep also creates sales order line items, where each line item identifies a product, quantity, sales price, ship-from location and the requested dates for shipment and delivery. When a line item's requested date cannot be met for a sales line, the system can suggest a date based on the delivery date control policy assigned to the line item. The item's inventory may also be reserved for a sales line in some scenarios. When all line items have been defined, the customer service rep generates a sales order confirmation and sends it to the customer.

Report Sales Order Picking/Shipping using the Basic Approach to Warehouse Management The shipping clerk typically uses the Release Sales Order Picking form to review and select open sales order lines that require picking/shipping, and then generate the picking lists for selected orders. This represents an order-based picking approach. The generation of a picking list will reserve the item's inventory for the sales line (if not already reserved), and the printed picking list identifies the reserved inventory. The warehouse worker reports actual picking against a sales order picking list. The shipping clerk reports actual shipment by posting the sales order packing slip for picked items.

Report Sales Order Picking/Shipping using the Advanced WMS Approach to Warehouse Management The shipping clerk typically uses the Release to Warehouse form to review and select open sales order lines that require picking/shipping, and then releases selected orders to the warehouse (which updates the release status for each order). With an order-based picking approach, the release-to-warehouse step can automatically create a shipment and load (with a waved status) and a shipment wave (with a released status) for each sales order. In addition, the released shipment wave automatically creates a picking work order consisting of work lines that identify the pick and put instructions. The work lines for picking identify the reserved inventory.

The warehouse worker uses the mobile device to report completion of picking work orders with delivery to an outbound dock, which results in a *ready to ship* status for the related shipment and load. The shipping clerk reports actual shipment by confirming the outbound shipments and posting the sales order packing slips for picked items.

Report Sales Order Picking/Shipping using a Simple Inventory Transaction The shipping clerk reports actual picking when posting the packing slip for a sales order. This simple inventory transaction applies to both the basic and advanced approaches to warehouse management, and it avoids the use of picking lists or picking work orders respectively. This option is not shown in Figure 7.1.

Generate the Invoice based on Sales Order Shipment The accounts receivable clerk periodically generates the sales order invoices based on information about which sales lines have been picked and shipped.

Enforce Steps in the Basic Model Several steps in the business process for sales order picking/shipping can be mandated by two item-specific policies. The first policy can mandate that picking must be reported before posting the packing slip for a sales order, and the second policy can mandate that the packing slip must posted before you generate the invoice for a sales order. These two policies -- termed the *Picking Requirements* policy and the *Deduction Requirements* policy -- are embedded in the Item Model Group assigned to the item.

Life Cycles related to Sales Order Processing The life cycles related to a sales order include a status for the header and each line item, a document status, and an inventory status for the item on a sales line. Steps in the business process automatically update the status. These steps are summarized in Figure 7.2, along with the status of related life cycles. The steps represent the essential touch points for updating status. A subsequent section provides an extended explanation of the status for each construct (Section 7.9)

Figure 7.2 Life Cycles related to Sales Order Processing

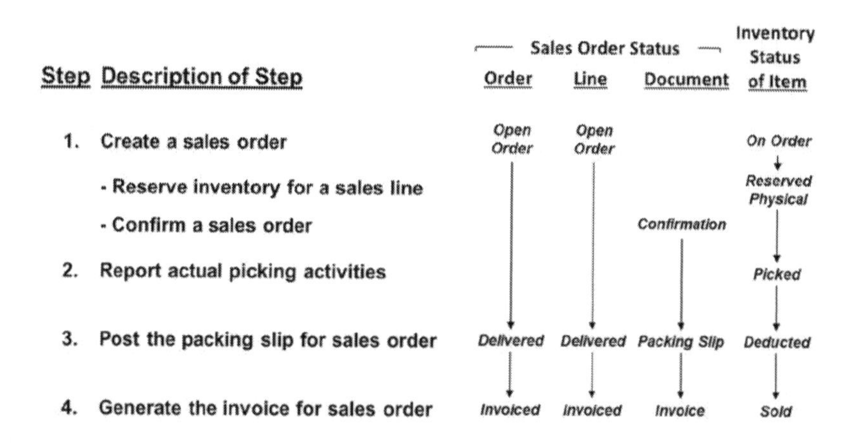

Different Approaches for Creating a Sales Order A manually entered sales order represents one of the common approaches for creating an order, and it was included in the basic model of sales order processing. The different approaches for creating a sales order are listed below. Steps within the basic model also apply to these other sources of creating a sales order.

- Enter a sales order for standard products or configurable products
- Create a sales order via release from a blanket sales order
- Create a sales order from a sales quotation
- Create a sales order for a replacement item related to an RMA
- Automatically create an intercompany sales order from an intercompany purchase order

Additional approaches to creating a sales order apply to retail-oriented operations and project-oriented operations, but these fall outside the book's scope. For example, you can enter a sales order using the call center capabilities, or you can enter sales orders and item requirements related to a project.

Other Types of Sales Orders You indicate the sales order type when initially creating a sales order. In addition to a normal sales order, the order types include a returned order. A sales order with a type of returned order is automatically created for an RMA (returned material authorization), and it handles the arrival, receipt and credit note for the returned goods (via a negative quantity line item). It also supports sending the returned item back to the customer.

7.2 Key Considerations for Sales Order Processing

Many of the variations in sales order processing can be supported by standard AX capabilities. Some of these can be viewed as major variations while others can be viewed as key considerations. This section summarizes a number of key considerations and the next section summarizes the major variations. A subset of these topics will apply to a given company. The following list of key considerations and their extended explanations represent a compendium of topics about AX capabilities. Each topic has been assigned an identifier for ease of reference, as shown below.

- A1: Assign a ship-from location to a sales order
- A2: Sales order quantity and UM
- A3: Assign sales order dates for shipment and delivery
- A4: Delivery schedule for a sales order line
- A5: Assign a sales price to a sales order line
- A6: Delivery address by sales order line
- A7: Totals for a sales order
- A8: Versions of a sales order
- A9: Reserve material for a sales order line

- A10: Identify sales-related backorders
- A11: Impact of changes to the sales order header
- A12: Indicate expediting for sales order picking/shipping
- A13: Place a sales order on hold
- A14: Impact of a customer hold and other types of stop flags
- A15: Sales order charges for freight

A1: Assign a Ship-From Location to a Sales Order A ship-from location consists of a site and warehouse, and it applies to the sales order header and line items. The default values for a sales order header can be inherited from the customer, where they typically reflect the nearest ship-from location. These values will be inherited by the line items unless item-specific defaults have been defined. The item-specific defaults for sales order shipments can be defined as a companywide or site-specific policy, where they typically reflect the preferred source or the sole source for the item. You can view alternative supply options (using the Supply Overview form) to identify inventory and scheduled receipts at different warehouses, an alternative item (if specified on the item master), and lead times to obtain the item from various sources. Another approach to analyzing supply options is available when using the new Dynamics AX, where you can access the Delivery Alternatives information to identify product availability for different ship-from warehouses and modes of delivery, and different product variants (if applicable).

The ship-from site and warehouse can have several impacts. The warehouse calendar can be considered when assigning ship dates, and the warehouse can be used for determining the transportation time to the customer address. They can affect sales order pricing and discounts, and also master scheduling logic about replenishment.

A2: Sales Order Quantity and UM An item's sales order quantity can reflect any authorized UM for the item. In many cases, the different values for an item's authorized UM will also be reflected in sales price trade agreements and/or sales agreements. In addition, an item's sales order quantity often reflects order quantity modifiers consisting of a minimum, maximum and multiple. They are defined in the item's default sales UM (if specified) otherwise they reflect the item's inventory UM. The order quantity modifiers are considered when manually creating or maintaining a sales line for the item, where a soft warning will be displayed when you enter a quantity that does not meet these criteria.

A3: Assign Sales Order Dates for Shipment and Delivery A sales order header has a requested ship date and a requested delivery date, where the difference represents the transportation time (termed transport days) between the ship-from warehouse and the delivery address. It also has a confirmed ship date and confirmed receipt date. The assignment of these dates are affected by the delivery date control policy assigned to the sales order header, which can enforce basic rules about applicable calendars (for the ship-from warehouse, the customer, and the mode of delivery), the expected transportation time to the customer address, and order entry deadlines.

A sales order line also has a requested ship date and delivery date as well as confirmed dates. These dates can be inherited from the sales order header, and changes in the header dates can optionally update information for the sales lines. However, the ability to assign a ship date and delivery date are impacted by the delivery date control policy for a line item, which is initially inherited from the specified item. A previous chapter provided further explanation about the delivery date control policy (Section 10.10).

A4: Delivery Schedule for a Sales Order Line A sales order line item normally consists of a single quantity and its associated ship and delivery dates. You can optionally specify a delivery schedule for a sales line, where each schedule line consists of a quantity and its associated dates. The total quantities within the delivery schedule lines must equal the quantity for the sales line, or the sales line quantity will be automatically adjusted.

A5: Assign a Sales Price to a Sales Order Line An item's sales price on a sales line can be assigned by several different approaches. The common approaches include a sales price trade agreement (Section 7.4) and a sales agreement (Section 7.5), where sales prices can reflect company-wide or site/warehouse-specific prices. Other approaches include the inherited sales price from a sales quotation or from copying a source document.

A6: Delivery Address by Sales Order Line Each line item inherits the delivery address from the sales order header, and it can be overridden. When printing a document such as a picking list or packing list, a separate document can be printed for each delivery address. The separate documents correctly communicate which line items are being sent to the delivery address.

A7: Totals for a Sales Order The system calculates several order totals, including revenue, cost and margin, discounts and taxes, and total weight and volume. Order totals can be displayed for order quantities, picked quantities, or shipped quantities.

A8: Versions of a Sales Order Posting a sales order confirmation results in automatic assignment of a version number. Each version is identified by the sales order number and a numeric suffix (such as -1 and -2). A sales order may be changed and the confirmation reposted in order to track versions of a sales order and communicate the changes to customers. The version number is displayed on a printed sales order confirmation. These historical versions can be viewed as part of inquiries about posted confirmations for a sales order. The system uses the existing sales order data (regardless of the assigned version number) for picking purposes and the related packing slip and invoice.

You can revert the existing sales order data to a previous version by using the *Copy from Journa*l function. You select from the displayed list of versions, and specify to delete lines from the existing order, so that the existing sales order data gets updated. You can optionally repost the sales order confirmation to assign a new version number.

A9: Reserve Material for a Sales Order Line Many scenarios employ reservations at the time you release a sales line for picking, and the picking list (or picking work) communicates these reservations. Some scenarios require reservations at the time of order entry, or reservations against an item's scheduled receipts.[1] Other scenarios sometimes require reservations of specific batches.

The reservation policy assigned to a sales order line item indicates whether inventory will be reserved automatically or manually. The options for this reservation policy include *Automatic* and *Manual.* A third option is termed *Explosion* and it supports automatic reservations of the components for a make-to-order product. When initially adding a line item, its reservation policy can be inherited from the item or from the sales order header. The reservation logic differs between the basic and advanced approaches to warehouse management.

A10: Identify Sales-Related Backorders A sales-related backorder within AX simply refers to any sales line with a ship date prior to a specified date (aka the backorder date).[2] This simple definition also applies to a sales line with an unshipped or partially shipped quantity, where the line has not been closed short when reporting actual shipment. This represents the more common interpretation of a sales-related backorder. Some scenarios need to identify the quantity for an

---

[1] The policy concerning reservations defaults from the sales order header, which defaults from a companywide policy embedded in the A/R parameters. An additional companywide policy determines whether reservations can be made against scheduled receipts.

[4] Two policies (embedded within the A/R parameters) indicate whether the system recognizes auto charges for the entire order and for line items.

unshipped or partially shipped line as "backordered" on sales order documents.[3] A standard inquiry provides information about sales-related backorders (labeled Backorder Lines, within Sales and Marketing).

The customer service rep typically reviews sales-related backorders and takes action for a selected backorder. The actions include updating the promise date or reducing the quantity for the sales order line. The rep can also request expediting of a supply order for the item.

A11: Impact of Changes to the Sales Order Header Several types of changes to the header information can optionally update sales lines. Examples include changes to the delivery date, delivery mode or ship-from location, and even changing the sold-to customer. You typically employ a prompt to confirm that changes in header information should change the sales lines. The use of a prompt (after changing selected fields in the header information) represents a companywide policy, where other values for this policy include automatic changes (without a prompt) and preventing the changes to line items.

A12: Indicate Expediting for Sales Order Picking/Shipping Several different approaches can be used to identify the need for expediting or prioritizing the sales order picking/shipping activities. The ship date provides the primary basis for scheduling these activities. It is frequently used in conjunction with other policies assigned to a sales order header or line item that indicate a priority or need for expediting, as summarized in Figure 7.3. The relevant fields can then be used as selection criteria when generating picking lists (or creating picking work) for sales orders.

- *Mode of delivery.* The mode of delivery often provides an organizing focus for picking/shipping activities, especially when preparing shipments for a scheduled pickup time. A delivery mode may reflect faster or expedited delivery, and can be associated with an Expedite Code.

- *Expedite code.* A user-defined Expedite code can be assigned to a sales order header and/or line item to indicate the need for expediting. In addition, you can associate an Expedite code with a mode of delivery, so that selecting the expedited mode of delivery also updates the Expedite code on a sales order.

Two of these expediting approaches – for mode of delivery and the expedite code – represent common business practices and merit further explanation.

---

[4] Two policies (embedded within the A/R parameters) indicate whether the system recognizes auto charges for the entire order and for line items.

Figure 7.3 Indicate a Priority or Expediting for Sales Order Picking/Shipping

<table>
<tr><th rowspan="2">Field Name</th><th colspan="3">Applicable Construct</th></tr>
<tr><th>SO Line</th><th>SO Header</th><th>Customer</th></tr>
<tr><td>Ship date</td><td rowspan="3">Yes</td><td rowspan="4">Yes</td><td rowspan="4">N/A</td></tr>
<tr><td>Mode of delivery</td></tr>
<tr><td>Expedite code</td></tr>
<tr><td>Sales order priority for fulfillment</td><td rowspan="2">N/A</td></tr>
<tr><td>Customer classification group</td><td>N/A</td><td>Yes</td></tr>
<tr><td>Shipping carrier/service</td><td>Yes</td><td>Yes</td><td>N/A</td></tr>
</table>

A13: Place a Sales Order on Hold Assigning a "hold code" to a sales order will prevent any further processing -- such as a confirmation, picking/shipping or invoicing -- while still allowing changes to the order. An additional policy for a hold code determines whether the reservations for a sales order (if any) should be removed after placing it on hold. In either case, the sales order demand will still be recognized by master scheduling logic. You create user-defined codes that represent variations of an order hold, and then select the relevant code when identifying a hold order. The hold for a sales order is identified by a "do not process" checkbox, by a hold icon in a list of sales orders, and by optional color coding when editing the order.

In the simplest scenario, you simply access the Order Hold screen from the selected sales order, and assign an order hold code. One or more hold codes can be assigned to a sales order. You can then clear the code after the hold has been resolved. The system automatically tracks the user and the date/time related to creation and clearing of a hold code. .

Some scenarios require an authorized user for clearing a hold code, such as the sales manager role for a hold code related to sales. You designate the authorized user as part of the setup information for a hold code, so that the hold code can be checked out and then cleared by the authorized user.

A14: Impact of a Customer Hold and other Types of Stop Flags The assignment of a customer hold for "all" transactions (as the policy for Invoicing and Delivery on Hold) will prevent new sales orders as well as transactions for existing orders, and result in a corresponding message. Other types of stop flags and restrictions can also be used. For example, the sales order transactions for an item can be stopped, or limited so a single site or warehouse. As another example, you can assign a stopped flag for a sales order line which will prevent updates to the sales line and the next steps such as picking/shipping.

A15: Sales Order Charges for Freight The charges related to freight or miscellaneous purposes can be manually assigned to a sales order, either as order-level charges or line item charges or both. A user-defined Charges Code identifies each type of charge and its related ledger account. The charges can be expressed as a fixed amount, an amount per piece, or a percentage of value. A fixed amount (for an order-level charge) needs to be allocated to the lines.

Some scenarios involve predefined agreements about charges, such as freight or handling charges for selected items or customers. An agreement about charges can be embedded in the sales price trade agreement information, or they can be specified separately as *auto charges*. These auto charges can be applied to an entire sales order or to individual line items, and expressed as a fixed amount, an amount per piece, or a percentage of value.

- *Order-Level Charges.* Charge agreements related to the entire sales order can be defined for a single customer, all customers or a group of customers (identified by the *Customer Charges Group* assigned to relevant customers). Examples of an order-level charge include order preparation costs for selected customers.

- *Line item charges.* Charge agreements related to the sales order line item can be defined by customer and item, such as charges for a single item, all items, or a group of items (identified by the Item Charges Group assigned to relevant salable items).[4] Examples of a line item charge include a setup fee for producing selected items for a customer.

When using the advanced approach to transportation management, the relevant charges can reflect the transportation costs associated with the sales order load (or the shipment or container) containing the sales order lines. These charges are automatically assigned to sales lines after confirming the outbound shipment.

---

[4] Two policies (embedded within the A/R parameters) indicate whether the system recognizes auto charges for the entire order and for line items.

7.3 Major Variations in Sales Order Processing

The basic model of sales order processing provides a foundation for covering several major variations. The explanation of variations related to sales trade agreements and sales agreements merit separate sections within the chapter. Other variations are summarized in this section, including the use of direct delivery orders, special orders, customer returns, sales quotations and performance metrics.

Direct Delivery Orders Some companies sell purchased items as a direct delivery order in addition to selling stocked products. One or more lines on a sales order can be designated as a direct delivery order, where each line requires creation of a corresponding purchase order (aka direct PO for short) for shipping to the customer address. Hence, a direct delivery order requires close coordination of sales order and purchase order processing.

There are two basic approaches for designating direct delivery for a sales order line. The first approach is typically performed by the customer service rep, who creates the direct PO for selected sales order lines. The selected lines inherit the sales order quantity and the item's preferred vendor and purchase price, and these values can be overridden prior to creating the direct PO. In the second approach, the customer service rep simply designates the selected line items for direct delivery (or the designation can be inherited from the item), and the purchasing agent subsequently reviews these designated lines (on the Direct Delivery form) in order to create and confirm the corresponding direct PO. The purchasing agent also reports vendor shipment of a direct PO, which automatically posts the packing slip for the corresponding sales order.

Special Orders Some companies sell purchased items as a special order in addition to selling stocked products. The material for a special order must be received and then shipped to the customer. One or more lines on a sales order can be designated as a special order, where each line requires creation of a corresponding purchase order (aka Special PO for short). Alternatively, you can start from an existing purchase order and then create linkage by selecting the applicable sales order. In either case, a special order requires coordination of sales order and purchase order processing, especially in warehouse activities to receive and immediately ship the material. This coordination of warehouse activities is commonly termed cross-docking.

Customer Returns and RMAs Customer returns generally require an authorization, termed a returned material authorization (RMA) number. In a simple situation, for example, the customer wants to return a defective product and obtain a credit. You create an RMA and provide the RMA number to the customer, who returns the item. You subsequently record the receipt of the returned item and create a credit note for the customer. RMA situations can become more complex with variations in handling a returned item, its replacement, and the related financial transactions.

RMA processing builds on sales order functionality. Each RMA has an associated sales order (termed the *return order*) for handling returns, and an optional second sales order (termed the *replacement order*) for handling replacements. Both sales orders have the same order number (but a different order type) with linkage to the originating RMA number.

- *Return Order.* Every RMA has an associated sales order (with a sales order type of return order) to only handle the arrival, receipt and credit note for the returned item. Creation of an RMA automatically creates the associated return order, which represents a mirror image of the RMA. Changes to the RMA information automatically update the return order; you cannot directly maintain data on the return order.

- *Replacement Order.* An RMA can have a second associated sales order when a replacement must be shipped to the customer. This replacement order can be created from the RMA to support immediate shipment, or created after a reporting arrival of an RMA line item (with a disposition code indicating replacement). This replacement order has all the functionality previously described for sales orders.

In many scenarios, the nature of the customer complaint is identified (via a case) before creating an RMA.

Sales Quotations A key step in many scenarios involves a sales quotation for the prospect or customer, where the sales quote can be converted into a sales order or identified as lost or cancelled. As a starting point, the sales rep often creates the sales quote from an opportunity. It can also be created directly or created from a selected customer, with an optional prompt to automatically create an associated opportunity.[5] Each quote line identifies a product, quantity, sales price, ship-from location and the requested dates for shipment and delivery. The sales price (and discount) can be automatically inherited from sales trade agreements. A quote line for a configurable product requires additional steps for using a product configurator to define a new configuration ID and calculate a suggested sales price.

---

[5] An opportunity can be automatically created for a sale quotation based on a companywide policy (on the Sales and Marketing Parameters form).

The customer service rep can perform price simulations as part of the process, and (if needed) identify the relationship between multiple related quotes. When information has been completely entered, the customer service rep sends the sales quote to the customer. The sales quote can be revised and resent, and the different versions of sent quotations are tracked. Based on the customer decision, the customer service rep indicates whether the sales quote has been accepted, cancelled or lost. An accepted sales quote can then be converted to a sales order, and (if needed) a customer can be created from a prospect.

7.4 Sales Prices and Trade Agreements

A sales trade agreement represents predefined information for selling products to customers, such as published list prices, customer-specific prices, and/or discount schemes. There are four types of sales trade agreements -- about the sales price, line discount, multi-line discount and total discount -- and further explanation focuses on the sales price aspects. The different types can be used in combination with each other, such as defining the sales price and a discount.

Sales Price Trade Agreements Sales price trade agreements provide the primary approach for defining a named price list for different groups of customers. Synonyms of a price list include a price book. A key construct -- termed the Price Group -- typically represents a named price list, such as a named price list for those customers representing Direct Sales or Distributors. Price groups are user-defined, and you assign a price group to relevant customers so that it is automatically inherited by sales orders for the customers.

Price trade agreements are expressed as multiple entries that identify the price group, the applicable items and their prices, and the effectivity dates. Other factors may include a different sales price based on the item's sales UM or for a quantity breakpoint on a sales order line. These factors affecting sales price trade agreement entries are summarized in Figure 7.4 and described below.[6] The following description focuses on the column labeled Sales Price and the use of the Price Group to represent a named price list.

- Pricing for a named price list as identified by the Price Group field. The price group typically reflects a group of similar customers.
- Pricing for a specific customer. The sales pricing can be for a specific customer, but a Price Group is still typically used to identify the named price list

[6] A set of companywide policies (embedded in the *Activate Price/Discount* form within A/R setup) determines whether the system recognizes these factors.

Figure 7.4 Sales Trade Agreements

	Factor	Sales Price	Line Discount	Multi-line Discount	Total Discount
Warehouse-Specific Information				N/A	N/A
Companywide Information					
			Types of Discounts		
Item	Item and UM	X	X	N/A	See item policy about including item value
Item	Group of Items	N/A	X Line Discount Group	X Multi-line Discount Group	N/A
Item	All Items	N/A	X	X	N/A
Sold-To Customer	Customer	X	X	X	X
Sold-To Customer	Group of Customers	X Price Group	X Line Discount Group	X Multi-line Discount Group	X Total Discount Group
Sold-To Customer	All Customers	X	X	X	X
Other Factors	Validity Period	X	X	X	X
Other Factors	Currency Code	X	X	X	X
Other Factors	Order Quantity Breakpoints	X	X	X	Order Value Breakpoint
Other Factors	Delivery Days Price Charge	X X	N/A	N/A	N/A
	Policies	Price Group Policy: Price includes sales tax			Item Policy: Include item value for total discount purposes

- ◆ Pricing with validity period, for supporting periodic price updates or seasonal price promotions. A companywide policy determines whether the sales price assignment reflects the order entry date on a sales order, or the requested ship date or receipt date for sales order lines.[7]
- ◆ Pricing by item and unit of measure, such as different prices per piece and per case.
- ◆ Pricing by currency type, such as separate pricing for foreign sales.
- ◆ Pricing with quantity breakpoints for the sales line quantity.
- ◆ Pricing based on delivery days. A higher price may apply for faster delivery, or the delivery lead time could vary by ship-from site/warehouse. However, the number of delivery days are normally defined as part of transport time between a warehouse and the customer's address, so that you normally the designate the "disregard lead time" policy as part of the entry.
- ◆ Pricing involves an additional charge, such as a charge for fast delivery, small order quantity or freight.

As noted earlier, price trade agreements are expressed as one or more entries that identify the applicable factors. A simple pricing scheme that represents this year's price list for Distributors, for example, would be expressed as one entry for each saleable item. Every entry would also identify the price group (representing the Distributor price list) and the effectivity dates. Additional

[7] You define this companywide policy as part of the A/R parameters about sales prices.

entries would be required for each site/warehouse when using site- or warehouse-specific pricing. Figure 7.4 illustrates the site/warehouse factor as a third dimension, since pricing for an item can be companywide or site/warehouse-specific (as defined by policies within the Storage Dimension Group assigned to the item).

During order entry, the price group assigned to the sales order determines the applicable trade agreement entries. This price group represents the named price list, and is initially inherited from the sold-to customer but can be overridden. The system uses the trade agreement information to automatically assign an item's price using the lowest price of applicable trade agreement entries.[8] The system also assigns the charge associated with the price if applicable. You can view available prices during order entry, such as viewing quantity breakpoints or future pricing to guide customer decisions.

Types of Sales Discounts in Trade Agreements The types of sales discounts can be related to a single line item, multiple lines, the order total value, or a combination of these approaches. These discounts can reflect one or more of the factors shown in Figure 7.4. Further explanation falls outside the scope of this essential guide.

7.5 Sales Agreements

Sales agreements define a commitment to sell products to a customer over a time period in exchange for special prices or discounts. Synonyms include a blanket sales order. The various types of a commitment include a total quantity for a specific product (with a specified sales price and/or discount percent), or a total value for a specific product, a category of products, or all products and categories (with a specified discount percent). After defining the sales agreement, you change its status from *on-hold* to *effective* in order to allow usage, such as creating sales orders linked to the sales agreement.

Types of Commitment for a Sales Agreement The type of commitment is defined in the header information for a sales agreement, which then affects the information for each line item, as summarized below.

- *Create a line item for a product quantity commitment.* You define the total commitment quantity and the sales price and/or discount percent for a specified item. An optional minimum or maximum release quantity may also be defined.

---

[8] The logic for finding the lowest applicable price requires an additional policy for each trade agreement record – termed the *find next* checkbox – otherwise the search will stop at the first applicable record.

- *Create a line item for a product value commitment.* You define the total commitment value and discount percent for a specified item. An optional minimum or maximum release amount may also be defined.

- *Create a line item for a product category value commitment.* You define the total commitment value and discount percent for a specified category of items. Section 3.1 (and Figure 3.3) previously explained categories and a category hierarchy for sales purposes. An optional minimum or maximum release amount may also be defined.

- *Create a line item for a value commitment.* You define the total commitment value and discount percent that will be applicable to all items or categories sold to the customer. An optional minimum or maximum release amount may also be defined.

As part of the header information, you indicate whether the maximum should be enforced on related sales orders. Additional terms and conditions may also be specified -- such as the payment terms and mode of delivery -- which will be inherited by related sales orders.

Linkage between Sales Orders and a Sales Agreement Several different approaches are used to link a sales order to a sales agreement, as summarized below. As a result of these approaches, you can view the sales orders linked to a selected sales agreement or generate the equivalent report.

- *Release a sales order from a sales agreement.* You create the sales order by starting from a selected sales agreement, and specify the item and quantity for a sales order line item. The sales order header inherits the terms and conditions from the sales agreement, and a line item inherits the applicable sales price or discount percent from the sales agreement.

- *Manually create a sales order linked to a sales agreement.* You specify the identifier of the applicable sales agreement when manually creating a sales order. The sales order header inherits the terms and conditions from the sales agreement, and a line item inherits the applicable sales price or discount percent from the sales agreement.

You can also unlink a sales order currently linked to a sales agreement, which means the sales price or discount percent for the line item will no longer reflect the sales agreement.

7.6 Customer Information

A subset of customer information directly relates to sales order processing. Each customer is defined in a customer master file by a unique identifier. Sold-to and bill-to customers require unique identifiers.[9] The following data elements have particular significance to sales order processing.

Preferred Ship-From Site/Warehouse Each sold-to customer can have a preferred ship-from site/warehouse which acts as the default value in sales order header information. The preferred ship-from location typically reflects the nearest location.

Ship-to Addresses A sold-to customer can have one or more addresses for delivery purposes, and a delivery address can be assigned to each sales order line item. When defining additional addresses, you can designate one as the default delivery address and others as alternates. During sales order entry, the system displays the default delivery address but you can select (transfer) an alternate to the order or create an order-specific delivery address. You can optionally designate (move) the order-specific delivery address as customer master information.

Bill-To Customer and Invoicing Considerations Each customer can optionally have a designated bill-to customer (termed the *invoice account* customer) that acts as a default on sales orders. The system supports a customer-specific numbering sequence for invoices. An invoice can be generated for each sales order or for multiple orders (e.g., with the same bill-to customer and currency) as a summary invoice.

Attributes Related to Pricing and Discounts The sold-to customer determines applicable pricing and discounts for a sales order. Sales prices in trade agreements can be based on the price group assigned to the sold-to customer. Discounts in trade agreements can be based on three other groups assigned to the sold-to customer -- the line discount group, the multi-line discount group, and the total discount group. A previous section described sales trade agreements (Section 7.4).

---

[9] The concepts of a sold-to and bill-to customer represent a basic viewpoint representative of many situations. The sold-to customer determines the applicable sales trade agreements, whereas the bill-to customer determines the applicable credit management policies. Each sold-to customer can have multiple delivery address (ship-to) locations which determine the applicable sales taxes. More complex situations often require additional information, such as the corporate entity associated with various sold-to customers, or the end-user associated with a delivery address.

Attributes Related to G/L Account Number Assignment General ledger account number assignments (such as revenue and cost of sales) can be based on a combination of customer and item characteristics. For example, the revenue account can reflect sales based on customer group and item group.

Financial Dimensions for a Customer The financial dimension(s) assigned to a customer provide a means to analyze sales by customer type. It can be used in conjunction with financial dimensions assigned to other entities -- such as items, sales campaigns and sales persons -- to provide multi-dimensional sales analyses.

One-Time Customers and Creating Customers during Order Entry When initially entering a sales order, the sold-to customer can be created on the fly by indicating a one-time customer. You enters the customer name and address information as part of creating the sales order, and the system automatically creates a new customer that is flagged as a one-time customer. Additional information defaults from an existing customer designated as the source of one-time customer information. The customer information can then be manually maintained, including the removal of the one-time customer flag.

Customer Hold Status A customer hold status (termed the *Invoicing and Delivery On Hold* policy) can prevent all transactions from being recorded, or just prevent shipments and invoicing to the customer.

Language for a Customer The language assigned to each customer determines which language version should be displayed on printed documents and other customer interactions. For example, the assigned language determines the language version for an item description on a printed packing slip or invoice.

Intercompany Trading Partner Some enterprises have multiple companies defined within a single Dynamics AX instance, and trading between the companies. A sister company can act as a vendor (or customer) for intercompany trading purposes. A vendor (or customer) must be defined that represents the sister company.

Customer Calendar of Work Days Assigning a calendar to a customer and related delivery addresses enables delivery dates to reflect the available hours of operation (when using the delivery date control capabilities). The delivery dates are based on the companywide calendar when a customer calendar is not specified.

Credit Management Policies The bill-to customer can have no requirement for a credit check, or a mandatory credit limit check with an associated credit limit amount. A companywide policy (embedded in the A/R Parameters) defines the basis for credit limit comparisons, such as the customer's current balance, shipments not yet invoiced, and open sales orders. You can check credit limit information during order entry, and the system prevents further transactions such as confirmations and shipments when the credit limit has been exceeded. A periodic task must be performed to enforce a credit limit consistency check on open orders when you change the basis for credit limit comparisons.

Summarized Information Summarized information about a customer can viewed, and transaction detail can be viewed by type of sales document such as outstanding quotes, sales orders, and return orders.

7.7 Performance Metrics Related to Sales Orders

Sales analysis can provide many of the performance metrics related to sales orders, and the multiple aspects such as items, customers and sales person. Additional metrics apply to shipping, such as on time delivery and full quantity delivery for sales orders. Each of these two metrics reflects several underlying assumptions, as described below.

- *On Time Delivery.* On-time delivery for a sales line reflects a comparison between the actual and promised ship date. The basis of the promised date can be the requested or confirmed date for the sales line, and either option should reflect consistent assignment of the promised date. In addition, achievement of on-time delivery typically reflects an exact match between dates or early delivery, so that only late shipments indicate a performance problem.

- *Full Quantity Delivery.* Full quantity delivery for a sales line reflects a comparison between the ordered quantity and the actual shipped quantity. The achievement of full delivery typically requires an exact match between quantities, so that quantity differences indicate a performance problem. Some would argue that delivery tolerances for over- and under-shipment quantities on a sales line (expressed as a percentage) should be considered in the performance metric.

You can identify these two performance metrics using a standard report or inquiry. An example report is labeled Top Sales Order Lines Not Shipped in Full or Not Shipped on Time. An example inquiry is labeled Deviations Between Actual and Expected Shipments.

7.8 Workspaces Related to Sales Orders

Several predefined workspaces are related to sales orders, as described in the following summary of each workspace and its applicable functionality.

Sales Order Processing & Inquiry Workspace This workspace summarizes several aspects of information about sales orders, and provides information for answering sales price inquiries. It identifies unconfirmed sales orders, orders on hold, delayed order lines, and partially shipped orders. You can create a new sales order, sales quotation or a return order, and create a new customer. For price inquiries, you can find the best sales price for a product (for a specified customer, date and quantity) and the associated discount if applicable. The links provide access to related information such as order events.

Sales Return Processing Workspace This workspace summarizes several aspects of information about return orders. It identifies expired orders and those that will expire within a week. It identifies the returns that have been registered as arrived. It also identifies open replacement orders. The links provide access to related setup information such as RMA disposition codes and return reason codes.

Master Planning Workspace This workspace identifies the sales order lines with a calculated delay so that you can respond appropriately, such as notifying the customer of the delayed delivery date or expediting the supply.

Prices and Discounts Workspace This workspace focuses on sales prices and discounts for retail purposes. However, it does cover the use of sales trade agreements and identifies those expiring within the next seven days.

7.9 Extended Explanation of Life Cycles Related to Sales Order Processing

The basic model of sales order processing (described at the beginning of the chapter) involves several key constructs and their life cycles, and Figure 7.2 illustrated these life cycles. This section provides an extended explanation about the status values for each life cycle.

Order Status An order status indicates the following steps in the life cycle of a sales order.

- *Open Order.* The status indicates the order has been created.
- *Delivered.* The status indicates all order lines have been shipped.
- *Invoiced.* The status indicates all order lines have been invoiced.

Line Status A line status indicates the following steps in the life cycle of a sales order line

- *Open.* The status indicates the line has been created, and partial shipment or invoicing may have occurred.
- *Delivered.* The status indicates the delivered quantity equals the order quantity. When using delivery tolerances, the delivered quantity can exceed the order quantity or a sales line with an under-delivery can be flagged as closed.
- *Invoiced.* The status indicates the line item quantity has been completely invoiced, taking into account the over- or under-delivery considerations.

Document Status A document status indicates the last document printed (aka posted) for the sales order, which includes the following documents.

- *Confirmation.* The status indicates the confirmation has been posted. Each time a sales order confirmation has been posted, a separate version of the confirmation is automatically created with a numerical suffix. You can view and print/reprint a selected version of a sales order confirmation.
- *Picking List.* The status indicates a picking list has been created, which represents the release for picking/shipping. A picking list only applies to the basic approach to warehouse management.
- *Packing Slip.* The status indicates the packing skip has been posted, which automatically creates a packing slip journal about the transactions. Each time a packing slip has been posted for a sales order, a separate version of the packing slip journal is automatically created with a numerical suffix. You can view and print/reprint a selected version of a packing slip journal. The packing slip journal also provides an option to cancel the associated transaction(s) or make corrections.
- *Invoice.* The status indicates the invoice has been posted.

Inventory Status The inventory status for the item on a sales line was shown on the right side of Figure 7.2. The steps in sales order processing will change this status from *on order* to *reserved physical, picked, deducted* and *sold.*

Released Status An additional status for a sales order -- termed the Released Status – only applies when using the advanced approach to warehouse management, and it reflects the release to warehouse step. It was not included in Figure 7.2. The released status of a sales order has the following significance.

- *Open.* The status indicates the sales order has not yet been released to warehouse for picking/shipping.
- *Released.* The status indicates that all sales order line items have been released to the warehouse for picking/shipping.
- *Partially Released.* The status indicates that some of the sales order lines items have been released to warehouse for picking/shipping.

After the release-to-warehouse step, the advanced approach to warehouse management involves several additional constructs for managing sales order picking/shipping. These include a shipment, load, wave and work orders, where each construct has a life cycle with different values for a status.

7.10 Additional Case Studies

Case 7.1: Analyze Delivery Alternatives for a Sales Order Line The customer service reps at a manufacturing/distribution company frequently encountered situations where the customer's requested delivery date could not be met. They needed to quickly assess product availability at different ship-from warehouses, for different product variants (if applicable), and for different modes of delivery in order to identify the options with the earliest delivery dates. They accessed the Delivery Alternatives information to support these order promising tasks. This approach allowed them to review the available options and select one as the basis for updating the promised ship date and delivery date on the sales line. In some cases, they opted to ship a smaller quantity than ordered (based on availability) and ship the remainder at a later date, which resulted in a delivery schedule for the sales line.

Case 7.2: Sales Quotations A manufacturing/distribution company typically created and sent a sales quotation to customers and prospects, and associated it with an opportunity (with a related win probability. The pipeline of sales quotations with a high win probability (above 90%) was used by master scheduling logic to drive supply chain activities. When the quote was accepted by the customer, it was converted to a sales order.

Sales quotations often involved negotiated prices. In these situations, the sales person employed price simulations (for individual lines or all lines) to evaluate the impact of a specified price, a discount percentage or a discount amount on the desired margins and contribution ratio. A price simulation could be saved with a user-defined description, and multiple scenarios could be saved, so that the sales person could optionally apply a saved scenario to the quotation.

Case 7.3: Automotive Tire Outlets A firm specializing in automotive tires required customized sales order processing to match the business processes at their outlets. The typical customer contact starts with a telephone inquiry about the options, pricing and availability about a given tire type, and proceeds through several steps including a quotation, sales order, work order and invoice. As part of the customizations for the quotation process, the system displayed alternative items with availability, pricing, and profitability along with highlighting to steer the customer's decision toward corporate promotions and higher margins. The system also suggested additional sales order line items about related services (such as tire installation and balancing) and indicated prior business with the customer. The quotation could be converted to a sales order and a work order with scheduling based on tire availability. When inventory was unavailable at the local outlet, the system checked availability across all outlets and recommended an inventory transfer, or generated a purchase order to the tire manufacturer. Many of the customizations represented work simplification and advanced decision support, with extensive prototyping to ensure ease-of-use, user acceptance and security considerations.

Case 7.4 Effective Use of Notes for Sales Orders Several roles within a manufacturing/distribution company used different note types (and note inheritance) in sales order processing, where notes were defined for the sales order header and/or line items. The applicable note types were printed on sales-related documents (such as confirmations, packing slips and invoices). Depending on the warehouse management approach, they were also printed on picking lists or displayed on mobile device transactions for sales order picking work, to indicate special instructions for the warehouse workers.

7.11 Executive Summary

Sales orders capture demands for the firm's products and service, and comprise a key element in the larger contexts of customer relationship management and the S&OP process. This chapter described a basic model of sales order processing, which provided the foundation for explaining key considerations and major variations. The chapter also covered customer information, performance metrics and workspaces related to sales orders. The case studies highlighted several aspects of sales order processing, such as quotations, delivery alternatives and notes.

Chapter 8

Purchase Order Processing

A primary responsibility of procurement is to coordinate and execute the supply chain activities driven by the firm's S&OP game plans. Procurement activities can significantly impact the firm's bottom-line performance in terms of reduced material costs and inventories, improved quality and lead time agility, and fewer disruptions stemming from stock-outs or delivery problems.

Purchase order processing for material represents a key business process within procurement, and often involves a wide spectrum of variations. As an explanatory approach, it is easiest to start with a basic model of purchase order processing. The basic model provides a foundation for explaining key considerations and major variations. Examples of major variations include the approach to purchase order pricing, the use of purchasing RFQs (request for quote), workflow approvals, returns to vendor, and coordination of procurement activities. These considerations are reflected in the following sections within the chapter.

1. Basic model of purchase order processing
2. Key considerations for purchase order processing
3. Major variations in purchase order processing
4. Purchase prices and trade agreements
5. Purchase agreements
6. Vendor information
7. Coordinate procurement activities
8. Metrics related to vendor performance
9. Workspaces related to purchase orders
10. Extended explanation of life cycles related to purchase order processing

8.1 Basic Model of Purchase Order Processing

The typical steps in purchase order processing can vary based on several factors, such as different approaches for creating an order and different approaches for purchase order receiving. This section summarizes a basic model of purchase order processing, as summarized in Figure 8.1 and described below. The section also identifies the related life cycles, the different options for creating a purchase order and the different types of purchase orders.

Figure 8.1 Basic Model of Purchase Order Processing

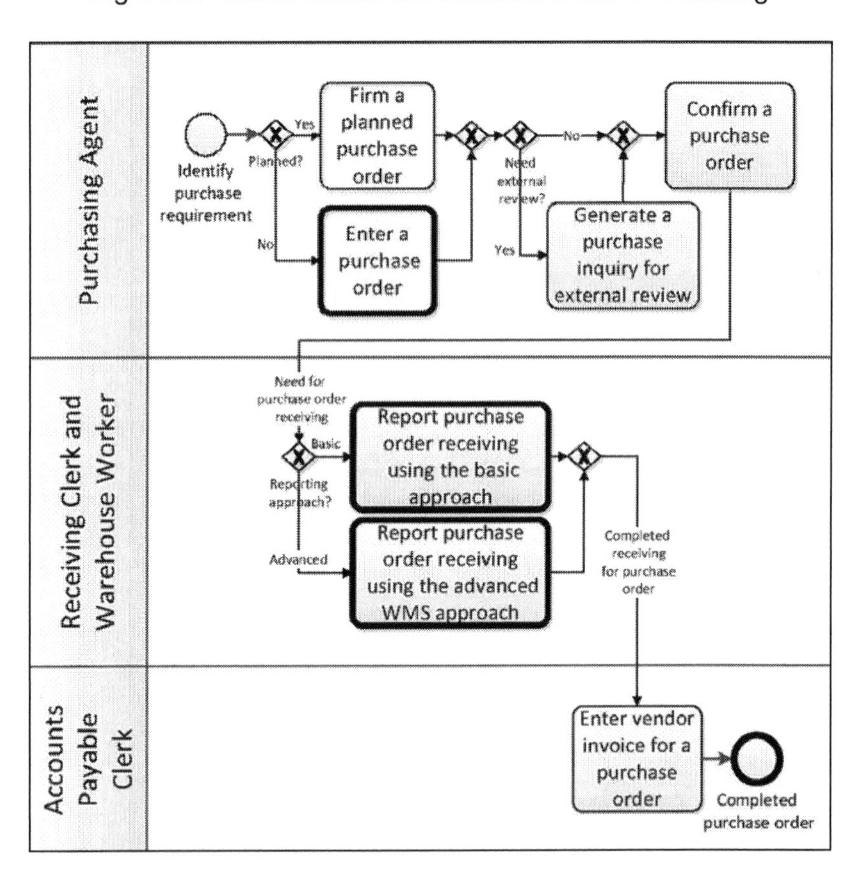

Overview of the Basic Model The basic model of purchase order processing consists of several steps performed by different roles, as summarized starts with the role of a purchasing agent and a requirement for purchased material. The requirement is typically identified by a planned order stemming from S&OP game plans and the item's planning data, and the planned order can be analyzed and firmed to create an actual purchase order. The purchasing agent can also manually enter a purchase order, typically as a result of an unplanned requirement. The purchasing agent can optionally generate a purchase inquiry for external review by the vendor. The purchasing agent confirms a purchase order when information has been completely entered.

A receiving clerk and warehouse worker perform subsequent steps for purchase order receiving, which differ when using the basic versus advanced approach to warehouse management. Some of the steps can be mandated.[1] An accounts payable clerk completes the process by entering the vendor invoice that typically reflects actual receipts.

Firm a Planned Purchase Order The purchasing agent typically uses the Planned Purchase Orders form to analyze and firm planned orders, which creates actual purchase orders with one or more purchase order lines based on grouping preferences.

Enter a Purchase Order The purchasing agent creates a new purchase order by starting from the Vendor form or the Purchase Order form (and using the Create Purchase Order dialogue), which results in a purchase order header. If needed, the rep maintains aspects of the header information, such as overriding information inherited from the vendor master. The purchasing agent also enters purchase order line items, where each line item identifies a product, quantity, purchase price, ship-to location and the delivery date.

Generate a Purchase Inquiry for External Review The purchasing agent generates a Purchase Inquiry in order to communicate the contents of a purchase order to the vendor, thereby providing the basis for external review before confirming the purchase order. Each generation of a Purchase Inquiry creates a history record so that you can view historical versions.

Confirm a Purchase Order The purchasing agent confirms a purchase order after completing the information, using either the Purchase Order form (for a selected order) or the Confirm Purchase Order form (for multiple orders satisfying the query criteria). The confirmed order can be sent to the vendor, and the confirmation enables subsequent processing steps such as receipts. Changes to a confirmed purchase order require an additional confirmation. Each confirmation creates a history record so that you can view historical versions of a purchase order.

---

[1] Several steps in the business process for purchase order receiving can be mandated by two item-specific policies. The first policy can mandate that item arrival must be registered before you can post product receipt, and the second policy can mandate that the actual receipt must reported before you can post the vendor invoice. These two policies – termed the *Registration Requirements* policy and the *Receiving Requirements* policy – are embedded in the Item Model Group assigned to the item.

Report Purchase Order Receiving using the Basic Approach to Warehouse Management The receiving clerk typically uses the Arrival Overview form to review and select open purchase order line items that require receiving, and then generate an arrival journal containing the selected lines. Alternatively, the receiving clerk can manually create an arrival journal, typically to handle an unplanned receipt. The receiving clerk registers the actual receipts against each journal line item and then posts the journal to update inventory balances. The receiving clerk also identifies the vendor's packing list number when posting the product receipt for a purchase order. For received material with putaway requirements, the warehouse worker uses the Transfer Journal form to report transfers from the receiving location to the putaway location.

Report Purchase Order Receiving using the Advanced WMS Approach to Warehouse Management The receiving clerk typically uses the mobile device to register a purchase order arrival into a receiving location (and assign license plate IDs), which automatically creates a work order for putaway. The warehouse worker uses the mobile device to report putaway from the receiving location to a stocking location. A suggested stocking location can reflect location directives, or the warehouse worker can determine and report the stocking location. Alternatively, the receiving clerk registers the arrival and reports putaway as part of a single mobile device transaction. In either case, the receiving clerk subsequently identifies the vendor's packing list number when posting the product receipt for the purchase order.

Report Purchase Order Receiving using a Simple Inventory Transaction The receiving clerk registers the item when posting the product receipt for a purchase order. This simple inventory transaction applies to both the basic or advanced approach to warehouse management, and it avoids the use of arrival journals and mobile devices respectively. This step is not shown in the figure.

Enter Vendor Invoice for a Purchase Order The accounts payable clerk uses the Posting Invoice form to record the vendor's invoice number and invoice information. The form can be accessed from the Purchase Order form, thereby inheriting information from the selected purchase order. It can also be accessed directly, which means that you must identify the applicable purchase order(s) for the vendor invoice. As part of the step, you indicate the quantity basis for initially populating the invoice information (such as the product receipt quantities) and whether to print the invoice.

Life Cycles related to Purchase Order Processing The life cycles related to a purchase order include a status for the header and each line item, and an inventory status for the item on a purchase line, where steps in the business process automatically update the status. These steps are summarized in Figure 8.2 along with the status of related life cycles. The figure also identifies the approval status and document status for a purchase order. A subsequent section provides an extended explanation of the status for each construct (Section 8.10).

Figure 8.2 Life Cycles related to Purchase Order Processing

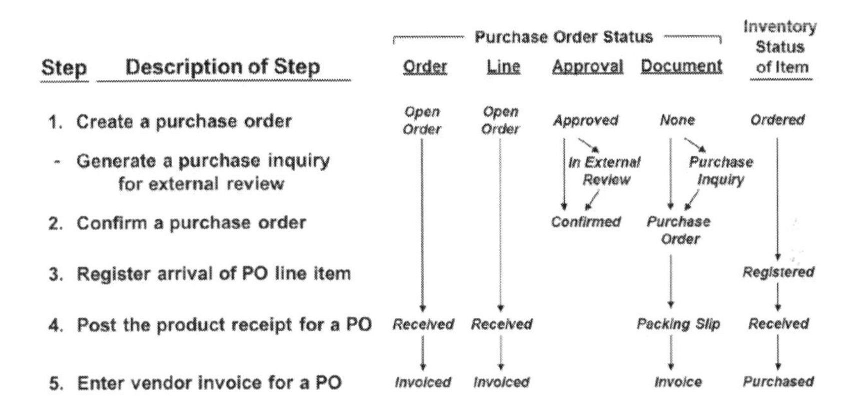

Different Approaches for Creating a Purchase Order The basic model identifies two common approaches for creating a purchase order -- by firming a planned order and by manual entry. Several additional approaches for creating a purchase order are listed below. The steps within the basic model also apply to these other sources of creating a purchase order.

- Create a purchase order via release from a blanket purchase order
- Automatically create a purchase order from an accepted reply to a request for quote
- Automatically create a direct delivery purchase order for a sales order, aka Direct PO
- Automatically create a purchase order from a sales order, aka a Special PO
- Automatically create a purchase order for a buy-to-order component of a production order
- Automatically create an intercompany purchase order from an intercompany sales order
- Automatically create a purchase order from an approved requisition

Other approaches to creating a purchase order apply to a project-oriented operation, such as entering a purchase order related to a project.

Other Types of Purchase Orders You indicate the purchase order type when initially creating a purchase order. In addition to a normal purchase order, the order types include a returned order and journal. A purchase order with a type of returned order is used for returns to vendor. A purchase order with a type of journal is typically used to define information about a possible purchase, and you change the order type to purchase order when ready.

8.2 Key Considerations for Purchase Order Processing

Many of the variations in purchase order processing can be supported by standard AX capabilities. Some of these can be viewed as major variations while others can be viewed as key considerations. This section summarizes a number of key considerations and the next section summarizes the major variations. A subset of these topics will apply to a given company. The following list of key considerations and their extended explanations represent a compendium of topics about AX capabilities. Each topic has been assigned an identifier for ease of reference, as shown below.

- A1: Purchase order quantity and UM
- A2: Alternative sources of an item's purchase price
- A3: Significance of a confirmed delivery date
- A4: Delivery schedule for a purchase order line
- A5: Totals for a purchase order
- A6: Versions of a purchase order
- A7: Impact of changes to the purchase order header
- A8: Identify potential problems in purchase order delivery dates
- A9: Identify purchase-related backorders
- A10: Impact of a vendor hold and other types of stop flags and restrictions
- A11: Purchase order charges for freight
- A12: Significance of Inventory Status for purchase order processing
- A13: Quality orders for purchase order receiving

A1: Purchase Order Quantity and UM An item's purchase order quantity often reflects order quantity modifiers consisting of a minimum, maximum and multiple. They are expressed in the item's default purchase UM (if specified) otherwise they reflect the item's inventory UM. The order quantity modifiers impact planned purchase order quantities. They are also considered when manually creating or maintaining a purchase line for the item, where a soft warning will be displayed when you enter a quantity that does not meet these criteria. The item's standard purchase order quantity also reflects considerations about order quantity modifiers, and it acts as a default value when manually entering a purchase line for the item.

An item's purchase order quantity can reflect any authorized UM for the item. In many cases, the different values for an item's authorized UM will also be reflected in purchase price trade agreements and/or purchase agreements.

A2: Alternative Approaches to an Item's Purchase Price An item's purchase price can be defined several different ways. As summarized in Figure 8.3, the four major approaches include a purchase agreement, purchase price trade agreements, the inherited purchase price from a source document, and a companywide standard purchase price.

Figure 8.3 Alternative Sources of an Item's Purchase Price

Source of Purchase Price on a Purchase Order		Factors	Significance of the Item's Purchase Price
Purchase Agreement	Purchase Agreement for a product quantity commitment	Committed quantity Minimum release quantity Validity period	Companywide or Site/Warehouse-specific Purchase Price
Trade Agreement	Purchase Price Trade Agreement	Vendor Unit of measure Quantity breakpoints Validity period	Companywide or Site/Warehouse-specific Purchase Price
Source Document	Purchase Requisition Accepted RFQ Reply Copy a Purchase Order	N/A	Inherit Purchase Price From Source Document
Standard Purchase Price	Manually Entered Standard Purchase Price Updated by Last Purchase Invoice	N/A	Companywide Purchase Price

As the simplest approach, an item's standard purchase price can be defined on the item master along with its default purchase UM. It represents a companywide purchase price that acts as the default on a purchase line when other sources of pricing information do not exist. This standard purchase price can be manually specified or automatically updated by the last purchase invoice.

As the second major approach, the purchase price can be inherited from a source document used to create the purchase order. Examples of a source document include an approved requisition, an accepted RFQ reply, and copying information into a purchase order.

The third major approach involves purchase price trade agreements, which can represent companywide or site/warehouse-specific purchase prices for an item. They can reflect different purchase UM, validity dates, and quantity breakpoints. A subsequent section provides further explanation of purchase trade agreements (Section 8.4).

The fourth major approach involves a purchase agreement, which specifies the item's purchase price based on a commitment quantity over a validity period. Releases against the purchase agreement create a purchase order, and the item inherits the specified price. Purchase agreements can also define a discount percent (rather than a purchase price), and a subsequent section provides further explanation (Section 8.5).

A3: Significance of a Confirmed Delivery Date Each purchase order line has a delivery date and a confirmed delivery date. The confirmed delivery date is initially blank, and should be updated to reflect actual conditions, such as a delayed delivery. Master scheduling logic employs the confirmed delivery date as the basis for suggested action messages and messages about calculated delays.

A4: Delivery Schedule for a Purchase Order Line A purchase order line item normally consists of a single quantity and its associated delivery dates. You can optionally specify a delivery schedule for a purchase line, where each schedule line consists of a quantity and its associated dates. The total quantities within the delivery schedule lines must equal the quantity for the purchase line, or the system will automatically adjust the purchase line quantity.

A5: Totals for a Purchase Order The system calculates several order totals, including a total amount, weight and volume. Order totals can be displayed for order quantities or received quantities.

A6: Versions of a Purchase Order Different versions of a purchase order can identify the history of changes. The system assigns a version number each time you confirm a purchase order, where the version reflects a numeric suffix to the purchase order number (such as -1 and -2). Hence, each confirmation provides a history of changes. The version appears on a printed purchase order confirmation, and the historical versions can be viewed and compared. The most recent version is used for master scheduling and the reporting of arrivals/receipts and vendor invoices. Two versions of a purchase order confirmation can be compared in order to identify differences.

A7: Impact of Changes to the Purchase Order Header Several types of changes to the header information can optionally update the purchase lines.

Examples include changes to the delivery date, delivery mode or ship-to location, and even changing the vendor. You typically employ a prompt to confirm that changes in header information should change the purchase lines. The use of a prompt (after changing selected fields in the header information) represents a companywide policy, where other values for this policy include automatic changes (without a prompt) and preventing the changes to line items.

A8: Identify Potential Problems in Purchase Order Delivery Dates The delivery date for a purchase order line provides the basis for expected receiving in the warehouse. In particular, the confirmed delivery date for a purchase line (or a line within a delivery schedule) typically indicates the most realistic up-to-date information from the vendor. Several standard inquiries identify potential problems about deliveries. You can identify purchase order lines without confirmed delivery dates or with past due delivery dates. You can also identify purchase-related backorders. These problems typically require action by the purchasing agent and coordination with the vendor, but they are also relevant for expected receiving activities in the warehouse.

A9: Identify Purchase-Related Backorders A purchase-related backorder within AX simply refers to any purchase line with a delivery date prior to a specified date (aka the backorder date).[2] This simple definition includes purchase lines with a partially delivered quantity, where the line has not been closed short when posting the product receipt. A partially delivered quantity is the normal interpretation of a purchase backorder. Standardized inquiries can be used to identify all purchase-related backorders or just those related to a vendor. The purchasing agent typically reviews purchase-related backorders and takes action for a selected backorder. The actions include expediting delivery from the vendor, updating the confirmed delivery date, and/or reducing the quantity for the purchase line.

A10: Impact of a Vendor Hold and other Types of Stop Flags and Restrictions The assignment of a vendor hold for "all" transactions will prevent posting of confirmations and product receipts and result in a corresponding message. As part of assigning a vendor hold (aka vendor status), you can optionally select a reason code and/or specify a release date. Other types of stop flags and restrictions can also be used. For example, the purchase order transactions for an item can be stopped, or limited to a single site or warehouse. The stopped flag for a purchase order line prevent further transactions until it has been removed.

---

[2] This simple definition is critical for understanding "backordered lines" with a future delivery date when compared to a specified backorder date in the future.

A11: Purchase Order Charges for Freight The charges related to freight or miscellaneous purposes can be manually assigned to a purchase order, either as order-level charges or line item charges or both. A user-defined Charges Code identifies each type of charge and its related ledger account. The charges can be expressed as a fixed amount, an amount per piece, or a percentage of value. A fixed amount (for an order-level charge) needs to be allocated to the lines.

Some scenarios involve predefined agreements about charges, such as freight or handling charges for selected items or vendors. An agreement about charges can be embedded in the purchase price trade agreement information, or they can be specified separately as *auto charges*. These auto charges can be applied to an entire purchase order or to individual line items, and expressed as a fixed amount, an amount per piece, or a percentage of value.

- *Order-Level Charges*. Charge agreements related to the entire purchase order can be defined for a single vendor, all vendors, or a group of vendors (identified by the *Vendor Charges Group* assigned to relevant vendors).

- *Line item charges*. Charge agreements related to the purchase order line item can be defined by vendor and item, such as charges for a single item, all items, or a group of items (identified by the *Item Charges Group* assigned to relevant purchased items).[3] Examples of a line item charge include a setup fee for purchasing selected items from a vendor.

When using the advanced approach to transportation management, the relevant charges can reflect the transportation costs associated with the purchase load (or the shipment) containing the purchase order lines. These charges are automatically assigned to purchase lines after confirming the inbound shipment.

A12: Significance of Inventory Status for Purchase Order Processing The use of Inventory Status only applies to WMS-enabled items, as described in a subsequent chapter about warehouse management (Section 10.2). A value for Inventory Status must be assigned to each purchase order line, typically with a value of *Available* or its equivalent in most scenarios. In some scenarios, the value for Inventory Status may indicate the grade or condition of the inventory being purchased (which may or may not affect purchase prices), or the need for receiving inspection.

A13: Quality Orders for Purchase Order Receipts A quality order can be automatically generated when you report purchase order arrival for an item, or

[3] Two policies (embedded within the Procurement and Sourcing Parameters form) indicate whether the system recognizes auto charges for the entire order and for line items.

when posting the product receipt, as defined by Quality Associations related to purchase orders for an item. A subsequent chapter provides further explanation of quality orders (Section 11.1).

8.3 Major Variations in Purchase Order Processing

The basic model of purchase order processing provides a foundation for covering several major variations. Two variations related to purchase prices are covered in separate sections about purchase trade agreements and purchase agreements. Other variations are summarized in this section, including the use of approved vendors, purchasing RFQs, purchase order approvals, receiving inspection, purchase order returns, direct delivery orders, special orders, buy-to-order components, subcontracted services and purchase requisitions.

Approved Vendors for a Purchased Item A purchased item can have one or more approved vendors, as defined on the Approved Vendor List for the selected item. You also define the start and expiration dates for an item's approved vendor. You can anticipate upcoming expiration dates using the Approved Vendor List Expiration form. The expiration date indicates when a vendor is no longer approved. An item's approved vendor represents a companywide policy.

Many scenarios need to enforce the use of an item's approved vendor, as defined by an item-specific policy labeled the *approved vendor check method.* This policy designates whether the approved vendor information will be ignored, prevent entry or provide a warning. The policy is initially inherited from the Item Model Group assigned to the item. Enforcement of the approved vendor policy applies to several situations. Examples include creation of a purchase order line for the item, defining purchase agreements, and the item's preferred vendor in coverage planning data.

Purchasing RFQs A request for quote (RFQ) provides a structured approach for soliciting and using purchase quotations for material items. The creation of an RFQ oftentimes starts with planned purchase orders and the intent of using a vendor reply to create a purchase order. A vendor reply can also be used to create purchase trade agreement entries. Other variations of an RFQ process involve different starting points and different intentions for using vendor replies. For example, an RFQ can be manually created with the intent of using a vendor reply to create a purchase order or a purchase agreement. An RFQ can also be created for a purchase requisition with the intent of updating the requisition status from *pending RFQ* to *pending completion.*

The use of purchasing RFQs requires an understanding of several key aspects of the AX conceptual model. As one key aspect, the terms *RFQ* and *vendor-specific RFQ* represent two different yet related constructs within AX. An RFQ has a unique identifier, and you create an RFQ to identify the items to be purchased and the applicable vendors that should be sent RFQ information. By sending the RFQ information, you create a vendor-specific RFQ (with its unique identifier) for each applicable vendor, and the vendor can reply to the vendor-specific RFQ. As another key aspect, you can create an RFQ for something that does not yet have an item number, and then assign the item number prior to accepting a vendor reply.

Workflows and Purchase Order Approval Some scenarios require a purchase order approval process when buying trade goods. An approval process is not typically required when purchasing trade goods based on requirements driven by S&OP game plans, as indicated by planned purchase orders. Within AX, an approval process does not apply to purchase orders that have been created by firming a planned order. Hence, an approval process only applies to a manually-created purchase order.

The term *change management* refers to use of an approval process for purchase orders. The associated policy -- termed *activate change management* -- can be companywide, vendor-specific or order-specific. Use of change management requires the definition of a purchase order approval process, which identifies the steps and responsibilities for approval. A detailed explanation of this setup information falls outside the book's scope because of book length considerations.

When an approval process applies to a manually-created purchase order, an approval status of *draft* is initially assigned to the order. This approval status automatically changes to *in review* after you submit the order for approval, and it subsequently changes to *approved* after successful completion of the approval steps. The status can then be changed to *confirmed*, as previously described in the basic model of purchase order processing (Section 8.1).

Receiving Inspection There are several variations of receiving inspection for a purchase order. For example, the inspection may be performed by receiving clerks at the time of reporting arrival, where the clerk can immediately assign an Inventory Status such as *Needs-Inspection* or *Damaged.* Alternatively, inspection may be performed after reporting arrival, where a quality control clerk reports test results against an automatically-created quality order. The test results may be reported while the material remains in a receiving location, or the material may be placed in a separate QC area until test results have been reported. Validation of the quality order can automatically update the Inventory Status of the received material, or the batch disposition status of a batch-controlled item.

Purchase Order Returns Returning material to a vendor typically involves a different type of purchase order (termed a returned order), but it can also be handled via a purchase order line item with a negative quantity. These two approaches are summarized below.

- *Purchase Order Type of Returned Order.* When creating a purchase order, you designate the order type as returned order and enter the vendor RMA (Return Material Authorization) number. The line items for a returned order are expressed with a negative quantity. Line items can be manually entered, or the original purchase order information can be copied precisely with an inverted quantity. A user-defined reason code (termed the *Return Action* code) can be specified for each line item. You can also indicate a line item does not warrant an actual return to vendor (via a scrap flag). After returning the item, the printed invoice reflects a credit note. A returned order for a purchased item can also be created as part of the process for handling customer returns.
- *Negative Quantity for Purchase Order Line Item.* A line item with a negative quantity can indicate a return to vendor, rather than using a separate purchase order type of returned order. The additional line item typically reflects situations where quality or delivery problems require an immediate return

Direct Delivery Orders A direct delivery order reflects a purchase order directly linked to a sales order, with material directly shipped to the customer. The previous chapter described direct delivery orders from a sales order viewpoint (Section 7.3).

Special Orders A special order reflects a purchase order directly linked to a sales order, with cross-dock receipts shipped to the customer. The previous chapter described special orders from a sales order viewpoint (Section 7.3).

Purchase Orders for a Buy-to-Order Component When the BOM for a manufactured item contains a buy-to-order component (identified by a component type of *Vendor*), a scheduled production order for the manufactured item automatically generates a linked purchase order for the component. The purchase order is automatically created for the component's preferred vendor (if defined) or the item's preferred vendor. The reference field information identifies the linkage in each order and the system reserves the scheduled receipt for the production order. Changes to the scheduled date for the production order can automatically update the schedule date for the linked purchase order (aka the reference order).

Purchase Orders for a Subcontracted Service A subcontracted service represents one example of a buy-to-order component and a key aspect of subcontracted production.

Purchase Requisition Purchase requisitions generally apply to many types of indirect materials or non-trade items, where procurement is triggered by a user request and involves an approval process before items can be purchased. However, a purchase requisition approval process sometimes applies to material items with requirements driven by S&OP game plans, such as sourcing a new item from a new vendor. The approval process employs the workflow management capabilities within AX, where you define one or more workflows for purchase requisition approval. A purchase order can be automatically created for an approved requisition.

8.4 Purchase Prices and Trade Agreements

A purchase trade agreement represents predefined information for buying material from suppliers, such as published list prices, negotiated purchase prices, and/or discount schemes. There are four types of purchase trade agreements -- about the purchase price, line discount, multi-line discount and/or total discount -- and further explanation focuses on the purchase price aspects. The different types can be used in combination with each other, such as defining the purchase price and a discount.

Purchase Price Trade Agreements A purchase price trade agreement indicates the purchase price for an item. The purchase price typically reflects one or more of the factors shown in Figure 8.4 and illustrated below.[4]

- Pricing by item and unit of measure, such as different prices per piece and per carton.
- Pricing by currency type, such as separate pricing for foreign purchases.
- Pricing with validity period, for supporting annual price updates or seasonal price promotions. The applicable validity period for assigning a price reflects the order date on a purchase order.
- Pricing with quantity breakpoints for the purchase line quantity.

[4] A set of companywide policies (embedded in the Activate Price/Discount form) determines whether the system recognizes these factors.

Figure 8.4 Purchase Trade Agreements

			Types of Discounts		
Site or Warehouse-Specific Information				N/A	N/A
Companywide Information					
	Factor	Purchase Price	Line Discount	Multi-line Discount	Total Discount
Item	Item and UM	X	X	N/A	See policy about including item value
Item	Group of Items	N/A	X Line Discount Group	X Multi-line Discount Group	N/A
Item	All Items	N/A	X	X	N/A
Buy-From Vendor	Vendor	X	X	X	X
Buy-From Vendor	Group of Vendors	X Price Group	X Line Discount Group	X Multi-line Discount Group	X Total Discount Group
Buy-From Vendor	All Vendors	X	X	X	X
Other Factors	Date Effectivity	X	X	X	X
Other Factors	Currency Code	X	X	X	X
Other Factors	Quantity Breakpoints	X	X	X	Order Value Breakpoint
Other Factors	Delivery Days Price Charge	X X	N/A	N/A	N/A
	Policies	Price Group Policy: Price Includes Sales Tax			Item Policy: Include item value for total discount purposes

- Pricing based on delivery days. A higher price may apply for faster delivery, pr the delivery lead time could vary by ship-to site/warehouse. However, the number of delivery days are normally embedded in the item's lead time for purchasing, so that you designate the "disregard lead time" policy as part of the entry.
- Pricing that involves an additional charge, such as a charge for fast delivery, small order quantity or freight.

Price trade agreements are expressed as one or more entries that identify the applicable factors. A simple pricing scheme that represents a single purchase price, for example, would require one entry for each item purchased from the vendor. Additional entries would be required for defining next year's price, quantity breakpoints, and variations in the items' purchase UM. Additional entries are also required for each site and warehouse when using site- and warehouse-specific pricing. Figure 8.4 illustrates the site/warehouse factor as a third dimension, since pricing can be companywide or site/warehouse-specific.

When manually creating a purchase order, or firming a planned purchase order, the trade agreement information will be used to automatically assign an item's price using the lowest price of applicable trade agreement entries. The system also assigns the charge associated with the price if applicable. You can view available prices during purchase order entry, such as viewing quantity breakpoints or future pricing to guide purchase decisions.

Types of Purchase Discounts in Trade Agreements Purchase discounts are calculated after the line item prices have been identified on a purchase order. The discounts can be related to a single line, multiple lines, the order total value, or a combination of these approaches. Further explanation falls outside the scope of this essential guide.

8.5 Purchase Agreements

Purchase agreements define a commitment to buy products from a vendor over a time period in exchange for special prices or discounts. Synonyms include a blanket purchase order. The various types of a commitment include a total quantity for a specific product (with a specified purchase price and/or discount percent), or a total value for a specific product, a category of products, or all products/categories (with a specified discount percent). After defining the purchase agreement, you change its status from *on-hold* to *effective* in order to allow usage, such as creating purchase orders linked to the purchase agreement.

Type of Commitment for a Purchase Agreement The type of commitment is defined in the header information for a purchase agreement, which then affects the information for each line item, as summarized below.

- *Create a line item for a product quantity commitment.* You define the total commitment quantity and the purchase price and/or discount percent for a specified item. An optional minimum or maximum release quantity may also be defined.
- *Create a line item for a product value commitment.* You define the total commitment value and discount percent for a specified item. An optional minimum or maximum release amount may also be defined.
- *Create a line item for a product category value commitment.* You define the total commitment value and discount percent for a specified category of items. The concept of product categories and a category hierarchy for purchasing purposes was previously explained in Section 3.1. An optional minimum or maximum release amount may also be defined.
- *Create a line item for a value commitment.* You define the total commitment value and discount percent that will be applicable to all items or categories purchased from the vendor. An optional minimum or maximum release amount may also be defined.

As part of the header information, you indicate whether the maximum should be enforced on related purchase orders. Additional terms and conditions may also be specified -- such as the payment terms and mode of delivery -- which will be inherited by related purchase orders.

Linkage between Purchase Orders and a Purchase Agreement
Several different approaches are used to link a purchase order to a purchase agreement, as summarized below. As a result of these approaches, you can view the purchase orders linked to a selected purchase agreement or generate the equivalent report.

- *Release a purchase order from a purchase agreement.* You create the purchase order by starting from a selected purchase agreement, and specify the item and quantity for a purchase order line item. The purchase order header inherits the terms and conditions from the purchase agreement, and a line item inherits the applicable purchase price or discount percent from the purchase agreement.

- *Firm planned purchase orders with grouping by purchase agreement.* You firm the planned purchase orders with grouping by purchase agreements, which results in a purchase order with multiple line items. Regardless of the grouping preference when firming planned orders, each resulting purchase order will inherit information from the applicable purchase agreement.

- *Manually create a purchase order linked to a purchase agreement.* You specify the identifier of the applicable purchase agreement when manually creating a purchase order. The purchase order header inherits the terms and conditions from the purchase agreement, and a line item inherits the applicable purchase price or discount percent from the purchase agreement.

You can also unlink a purchase order currently linked to a purchase agreement, which means the purchase price or discount percent for the line item will no longer reflect the purchase agreement.

8.6 Vendor Information

A subset of vendor information directly relates to purchase order processing. Each vendor is defined in a vendor master file by a unique identifier. Buy-from and pay-to vendors require unique identifiers, and a buy-from vendor can optionally have one or more ship-from addresses. The following data elements have particular significance to purchase order processing.

Vendor Calendar of Work Days When purchase lead times are expressed in working days, the calculation of a purchase order start date and/or delivery date can be based on a specified calendar of the vendor's working days. The calculations use the companywide calendar as the default when a vendor calendar is not specified.

Language for a Vendor The language assigned to each vendor determines which language version should be displayed on printed documents and other vendor interactions. For example, the assigned language determines the language version for an item description on a purchase order confirmation.

Attributes Related to G/L Account Number Assignment General ledger (G/L) account number assignments (such as trade payables and purchase price variances) are based on a combination of vendor and item characteristics. For example, the trade payables account updated by a purchase order receipt can be based on the vendor group and item group assigned to the vendor and item respectively.

Financial Dimensions for a Vendor The financial dimension(s) assigned to a vendor provide a means to analyze purchases by vendor type. They can be used in conjunction with financial dimensions assigned to other entities such as items to provide multi-dimensional purchase analyses.

One-Time Vendors and Creating Vendors during Purchase Order Entry When initially entering a purchase order, the buy-from vendor can be created on the fly by indicating a one-time vendor. You enter the vendor name and address information as part of creating the purchase order, and the system automatically creates a new vendor that is flagged as a one-time vendor. Additional information defaults from an existing vendor designated as the source of one-time vendor information. The vendor information can then be manually maintained, including the removal of the one-time vendor flag.

Vendor Hold Status A vendor hold status can prevent all transactions from being recorded, or only prevent invoices or payments from being entered for the vendor. You assign the vendor hold status by explicitly accessing the *change vendor status* function from the vendor master. Optional information about the hold status includes a hold release date and the assignment of a user-defined reason code. An additional policy only applies to a multi-company scenario (in which the same vendor has been defined in multiple AX companies within one AX instance), so that you can optionally assign the vendor's hold status to all companies.

Same Vendor defined for Multiple Companies Some multi-company scenarios involve the same vendor serving multiple companies. In this case, you can define the vendor in one company, and then add the vendor to another company along with an applicable vendor group and vendor hold status. However, you must define all other aspects of vendor information in each additional company.

Intercompany Trading Partner Some enterprises have multiple companies defined within a single Dynamics AX instance, and trading between the companies. A sister company can act as a vendor (or customer) for intercompany trading purposes. A vendor (or customer) must be defined that represents the sister company. A subsequent chapter explains intercompany orders (Chapter 18).

Summarized Information by Vendor Summarized information about a vendor can be viewed, and transaction detail can be viewed by type of purchase document, such as outstanding purchase orders, receipts, invoices, and backorder purchase lines.

8.7 Coordinate Purchase Orders

A firm's S&OP game plans provide the primary driver of purchasing activities for material items. The key tools for coordinating these activities include planned purchase orders and action messages, which reflect the model of SCM decision-making embedded in coverage planning data for purchased items (Section 9.3). Several other coordination tools can also be employed, such as calculated delay messages and the inquiries/reports about problems in delivery dates.

Planned Purchase Orders The planned orders can be viewed on the Planned Purchase Orders form or the Planned Orders form, where the displayed information typically represents the current master plan.[5] Planned orders can be viewed based on selection criteria such as the buyer group and order date, so that the responsible buyer can mark and firm the planned orders accordingly.

Actual purchase orders can be created from planned orders via a function termed *firming planned orders*. You typically mark (via a check box) the planned orders needing to be firmed. The firming function creates single-line purchase orders

[5] You can view information based on a selected set of master plan data or forecast plan data. For simplicity's sake the explanation focuses on the set of data representing the current master plan.

unless you indicate grouping preferences via the firming dialogue.[6] For example, the grouping preferences can reflect the vendor, a period size (such as daily or weekly) and purchase agreements, resulting in a multi-line purchase order with all lines related to the same purchase agreement. Execution of the firming function automatically deletes the selected planned orders, and creates a log for tracking which planned orders have been firmed and by whom.

In many cases, you may need to analyze the rationale for a planned purchase order prior to firming. You can view the net requirements and related action messages for a selected planned order. The analysis may lead to one or more actions. For example, you may select a different vendor, change the suggested quantity or delivery date, and/or convert the planned order to a purchasing RFQ.

Action Messages Action messages represent one of the key tools for coordinating procurement activities to meet the S&OP game plans. Master scheduling logic can generate action messages for planned and actual purchase orders. The logic reflects the action message policies embedded within the coverage group assigned to an item, as described in a previous chapter (Section 9.10). The action messages can be viewed and acted upon in several different ways. For example, you can view action messages on the Actions form, and optionally apply the suggested action for a selected message by accessing the Action Graph.

Messages about Calculated Delays This message indicates that a purchase order delivery date will cause a delay in meeting a requirement date, and the purchase order typically has an associated "advance" action message. The messages can be viewed from several different starting points (such as the Net Requirements inquiry) and you can access the relevant purchase order to indicate a change.

Identify Potential Problems in Delivery Dates The confirmed delivery date for a purchase line (or a line within a delivery schedule) typically indicates the most realistic up-to-date information from the vendor. A standard inquiry identifies confirmed purchase orders without confirmed delivery dates, and a second inquiry identifies purchase lines with past due delivery dates. You can also identify purchase-related backorders. These problems typically require action by the purchasing agent and coordination with the vendor.

[6] The default values for grouping preferences (when firming planned purchase orders) are defined as part of the Master Planning parameters.

8.8 Metrics Related to Vendor Performance

Several different metrics can indicate vendor performance. Example metrics within standard AX include on-time delivery of purchase orders, returns to vendor, and purchase price variances for standard cost items. Other metrics reflect a quality perspective, such as failed quality orders for purchase receipts, and purchasing-related cases. Another source of metrics involves user-definable evaluation criteria, and the manual assignment of a rating for a vendor. These various types of performance metrics are described below. Some scenarios require customized metrics, as illustrated in Case 8.1.

- *Review on-time delivery of purchase orders.* Example metrics for a given vendor include the percent of on-time receipts (and the percent late and percent early), and the average days late (and average days early).
- *Review returns to vendor.* Purchase order returns to a vendor can be viewed in units or value.
- *Review purchase price variances for standard cost items.* With a standard cost item, you can review purchase price variances related to purchase orders and vendor invoices.
- *Review failed quality orders related to purchase receipts.* When using quality orders, you can review the purchasing-related quality orders that have failed the validation of test results.
- *Review cases related to purchase orders or vendors.* When using cases, you can review the cases related to purchase orders or vendors.
- *Review the ratings assigned to user-definable vendor evaluation criteria.* The user-definable criteria can reflect any metric, and you manually assign the vendor's rating for each metric. The rating consists of a 5-point scale ranging from 1 (very poor) to 5 (very good).
- *Review vendor replies to RFQs.* The primary metric involves a comparison between the number of RFQs sent to the vendor versus the number of accepted replies (and rejected replies), where the numbers reflect a specified time interval. A higher ratio between the numbers of accepted replies versus sent RFQs indicates better performance.

8.9 Workspaces Related to Purchase Orders

Several predefined workspaces are related to purchase orders, as described in the following summary of each workspace and its applicable functionality.

Purchase Order Preparation Workspace This workspace identifies purchase orders with a status of "In External Review" or "Approved", and the order lines without a confirmed delivery date. You can confirm orders and create new purchase orders. The displayed information can be filtered for a selected buyer group. The links provide access to information about planned purchase orders and the RFQ replies from vendors.

Purchase Order Receipt and Follow-up Workspace This workspace identifies purchase lines with delayed receipts and with pending receipts, and registered arrivals that still need posting of the product receipt. It also identifies order receipts where the vendor invoice has not yet been entered. The links provide access to information about open purchase order lines, the product receipt journal, and the Direct Delivery form (for coordinating direct delivery orders).

Master Planning Workspace This workspace identifies the planned purchase orders, and also the action messages and calculated delay messages about purchase orders.

8.10 Extended Explanation of Life Cycles Related to Purchase Order Processing

The basic model of purchase order processing (described at the beginning of the chapter) involves several key constructs and their life cycles, and Figure 8.2 illustrated these life cycles. This section provides an extended explanation about the status values for each life cycle.

Order Status An order status indicates the following steps in the life cycle of a purchase order.

- *Open Order*. The status indicates the order has been created.
- *Delivered*. The status indicates all order lines have a delivered status.
- *Invoiced*. The status indicates all order lines have an invoiced status.
- *Cancelled*. The status indicates the purchase order has been cancelled.

Line Status A line status indicates the following steps in the life cycle of a purchase order line, or a line within the delivery schedule for a purchase order line.

- *Open Order*. The status indicates the line has been created, and partial receipts or invoices may have been entered.
- *Delivered*. The status indicates that the delivered quantity equals the order quantity. When using delivery tolerances, the delivered quantity can exceed

the order quantity or the under-delivery can be flagged as closed when posting the product receipt.

- *Invoiced.* The status indicates the line item quantity has been completely invoiced, taking into account the over- or under-delivery considerations mentioned above.
- *Cancelled.* The status indicates the purchase order has been cancelled, and the quantity not yet registered or received will be cancelled.

Document Status A document status indicates the last document posted for the purchase order, as described below.

- *None.* The status indicates that a confirmation or purchase inquiry has not been posted for the purchase order.
- *Purchase Inquiry.* The status indicates a purchase inquiry has been posted.
- *Purchase Order.* The status indicates a purchase order confirmation has been posted.
- *Packing Slip.* The status indicates a product receipt has been posted for all lines.
- *Invoiced.* The status indicates the vendor's invoice has been posted.

Approval Status The purchase order approval status indicates whether a purchase inquiry and/or a confirmation have been posted for the order, as described below.

- *Approved.* The status indicates the purchase order needs to be confirmed.
- *In External Review.* The status indicates a purchase inquiry has been posted for the order.
- *Confirmed.* The status indicates the purchase order confirmation has been posted, so that subsequent steps (such as receiving) can be reported.

Additional values pertain to purchase orders requiring an approval process, as described below.

- *Draft.* The status indicates creation of a purchase order that must go through an approval process, where the purchase order has not yet been submitted for approval.
- *In Review.* The status indicates a purchase order going through an approval process, where the order has been submitted but not yet approved.

Inventory Status The inventory status for the item on a purchase line was shown on the right side of Figure 8.2, and the steps in purchase order processing will change this status from *ordered* to *registered, received* and *purchased.*

8.11 Additional Case Studies

Case 8.1: Vendor Performance Metrics A manufacturing company wanted to customize the vendor performance metrics within standard AX. One metric involved complete delivery quantity for purchase lines during a specified time period, where the metric reflected a comparison of actual quantity received versus the ordered quantity. The metric consisted of three categories for (1) exact quantity, (2) under-delivery within delivery tolerance, and (3) over-delivery within tolerance. Another metric involved purchase receipts of items requiring a certificate of analysis from the vendor, where the metric indicated whether the COA was included with the receipt.

Case 8.2: Indicate Inspection Requirements using Inventory Status The Inventory Status value of *Needs-Inspection* was assigned to purchase lines for items requiring inspection, thereby communicating the need for inspection when reporting purchase order arrival. A given item that always requires inspection was assigned a default value of *Needs-Inspection* for each supplying vendor (using the Default Item Status form). In this way, the value will be inherited when creating a purchase order line or firming a planned order. The quality control clerk changed the value of Inventory Status after inspecting the received material, such as changing the value to *Available* or *Damaged*.

Case 8.3 Effective Use of Notes for Purchase Orders Several different note types (and note inheritance) were used in purchase order processing, where notes were defined for the purchase order header and/or line items. The applicable note types were printed on purchase-related documents such as confirmations. They were also displayed on mobile device transactions for reporting purchase order arrival, thereby indicating special instructions for the receiving clerk.

8.12 Executive Summary

Purchase order processing for direct material often involves a wide spectrum of business practices. This chapter described a basic model for purchase order processing, which provided the foundation for explaining key considerations and major variations. It covered sourcing and agreement information for purchased items, including approved vendors and agreements about purchase prices. Master scheduling logic can help coordinate procurement activities by communicating the need for planned orders and suggested changes to existing orders. Several metrics apply to vendor performance, and workspaces provide insights about procurement activities.

Chapter 9

Transfer Order Processing

Many businesses involved in manufacturing and distribution have inventory at multiple physical sites, and require transfers between these sites. Transfers between sites can be managed using transfers orders or intercompany orders, depending on the grouping of physical sites into companies. This chapter focuses on transfer orders for coordinating transfers between inventory locations in a single company. As an explanatory approach, it is easiest to start with a basic model of transfer order processing. The basic model provides a foundation for explaining key considerations and coordination of transfer orders. These considerations are reflected in the following sections within the chapter.

1. Basic Model of Transfer Order Processing
2. Key Considerations about Transfer Order Processing
3. Coordinate Transfer Order Activities

9.1 Basic Model of Transfer Order Processing

The typical steps in transfer order processing can vary based on several factors, such as different approaches to warehouse management at the ship-from and ship-to warehouses. This section summarizes a basic model of transfer order processing and the related life cycles.

Overview of the Basic Model The basic model of transfer order processing starts with a requirement to transfer material, and the role of a purchasing agent or DRP coordinator.[1] This explanation primarily employs a role title of DRP coordinator. The requirement is typically identified by a planned order stemming from S&OP game plans and the item's planning data, and the planned order can

[1] The role title of a DRP coordinator is not specifically identified within the standard AX roles. Similar titles within the standard AX roles include the logistics manager, transportation coordinator and warehouse planner.

be analyzed and firmed to create an actual transfer order. A planned transfer order can also be manually entered (and optionally approved) and then firmed, or an actual transfer order can be manually entered. These manual entries often stem from unplanned requirements. At the ship-from warehouse, a warehouse worker and shipping clerk perform subsequent steps for transfer order picking/shipping, which differ when using the basic versus advanced approach to warehouse management. Both approaches support order-based picking described in this basic model. After actual shipment, an item's inventory is moved to the in-transit warehouse associated with the ship-from warehouse, and receipts reduce the in-transit inventory.

At the ship-to warehouse, a receiving clerk and warehouse worker perform subsequent steps for transfer order receiving, which differ when using the basic versus advanced approach to warehouse management. These roles and steps are summarized in Figure 9.1 and described below.

Figure 9.1 Basic Model of Transfer Order Processing

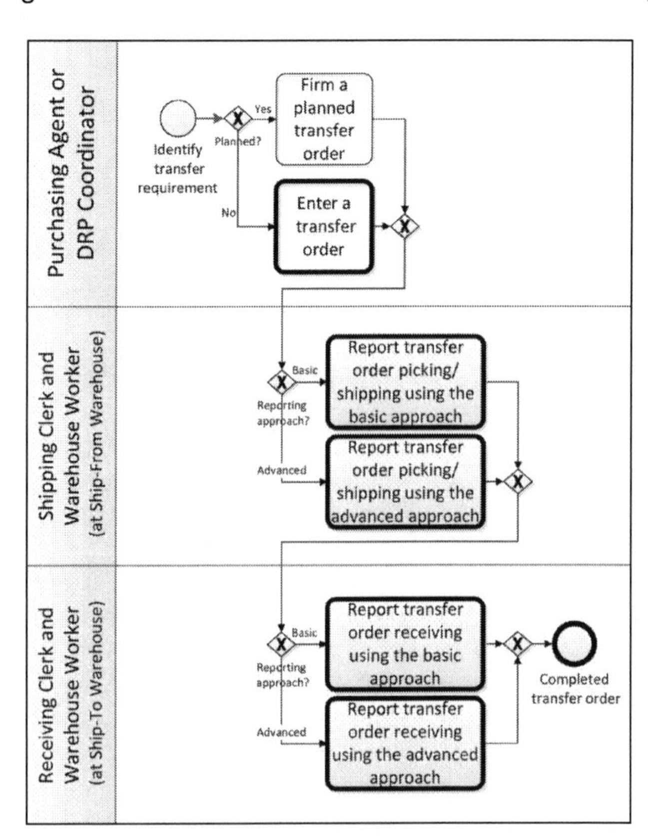

Firm a Planned Transfer Order The purchasing agent or DRP coordinator typically uses the Planned Transfer Orders form to analyze and firm planned orders, which creates actual transfer orders with one or more transfer order lines based on grouping preferences.

Enter a Transfer Order The purchasing agent or DRP coordinator creates a new transfer order by starting from the Transfer Order form and specifying the ship-from and ship-to warehouses (and the dates for shipment and receipt) as part of the transfer order header. The DRP coordinator also enters transfer order line items, where each line item identifies a product, a quantity, and the shipment and receipt dates.

Report Transfer Order Picking/Shipping using the Basic Approach to Warehouse Management The shipping clerk typically uses the Release Transfer Order Picking form to review and select open transfer order lines that require picking/shipping, and then generate the picking lists for selected orders. The generation of a picking list will reserve the item's inventory for the transfer line (if not already reserved). As alternative approaches, a picking list can be generated from a transfer order, or the picking lists can be generated from a periodic task.

The warehouse worker reports actual picking against a transfer order picking list and then posts it. The shipping clerk reports actual shipment by posting the transfer order shipment for picked items.

Report Transfer Order Picking/Shipping using the Advanced Approach to Warehouse Management In a typical scenario, the shipping clerk uses the Release To Warehouse form to review and select open transfer order lines that require picking/shipping, and then releases selected orders to the warehouse (which updates the release status for each order). With an order-based picking approach, the release-to-warehouse step can automatically create a shipment and load (with a waved status) and a shipment wave (with a released status) for each transfer order. In addition, the released shipment wave automatically creates a picking work order consisting of work lines that identify the pick and put instructions.

The warehouse worker reports actual picking by using the mobile device to report completion of picking work orders. Completion of the picking work to an outbound dock results in shipments and loads that are ready to ship. The shipping clerk reports actual shipment by confirming the outbound shipments.

Report Transfer Order Picking/Shipping using a Simple Inventory Transaction The shipping clerk can use the Transfer Order form to simply report actual shipment of the transfer order, where the relevant details about the picked inventory (such as bin location and possibly the license plate ID) must be identified for each transfer order line item prior to posting. This simple inventory transaction works for both the basic and advanced approach to warehouse management. It avoids the use of picking lists in the basic approach, and it avoids the use of picking work orders (and the use of loads, shipments and waves) in the advanced approach. This option is not shown in Figure 9.1 in order to simplify the diagram.

Review In-Transit Inventory for an Item You can view an item's in-transit inventory on various on-hand inquiries, or view the on-hand inquiries for the in-transit warehouse.

Report Transfer Order Receiving using the Basic Approach to Warehouse Management The receiving clerk typically uses the Arrival Overview form to review and select shipped transfer order lines, and then create an arrival journal containing the selected lines. The receiving clerk registers the actual receipts against each journal line item and posts the journal to update inventory balances. As a final step, the receiving clerk posts the receipt for a transfer order. For received material with putaway requirements, the warehouse worker uses the Transfer Journal form to report transfers from the receiving location to the putaway location.

Report Transfer Order Receiving using the Advanced Approach to Warehouse Management The nature of transfer order receiving depends on whether the shipped material has been identified with a license plate ID. In a typical process, the receiving clerk uses the mobile device to receive a license plate ID for a transfer order shipment, which updates inventory balances and automatically creates putaway work. The warehouse worker uses the mobile device to report putaway from the receiving location to a stocking location. A suggested stocking location can reflect location directives, or the warehouse worker can determine and report the stocking location. As an alternative reporting approach, the receiving clerk can report receipt and putaway as part of a single mobile device transaction.

When the shipped material is not identified with a license plate ID, the receiving clerk uses the mobile device to receive a transfer order number, and subsequent receiving steps are the same.

Report Transfer Order Receiving using a Simple Inventory Transaction A simple inventory transaction applies when using the basic approach to warehouse management. The receiving clerk can use the Transfer Order form to simply post the transfer order receipt, and avoid the use of arrival journals. When using the advanced approach to warehouse management, this simple inventory transaction becomes quite complicated so that it does not represent a useful alternative. The option for a simple inventory transaction is not shown in Figure 9.1 in order to simplify the diagram.

Life Cycles Related to Transfer Order Processing The life cycles related to the basic model of transfer order processing include a status for the transfer order, and an inventory status for the item on a transfer order line, where steps in the business process automatically update the status. These steps are summarized in Figure 9.2, along with the status of related life cycles. The steps represent the essential touch points for updating status.

Figure 9.2 Life Cycles Related to Transfer Order Processing

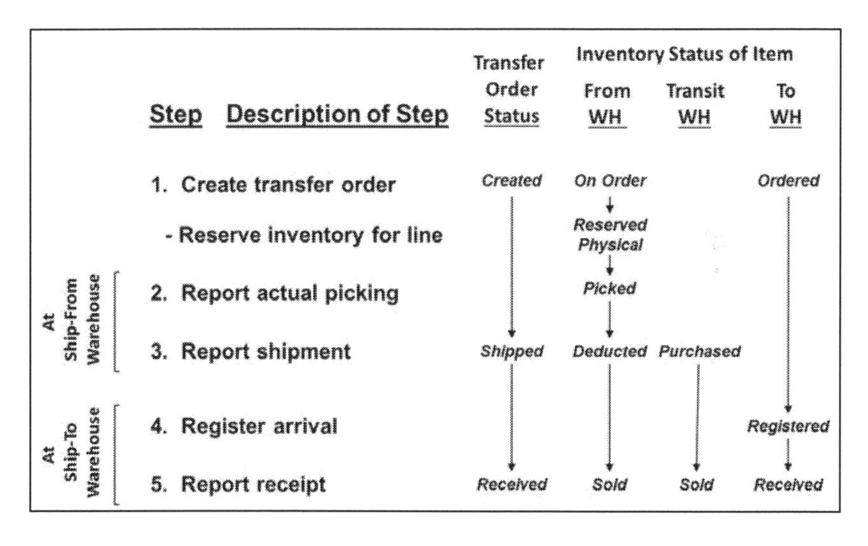

An order status indicates the following steps in the life cycle of a transfer order.

- *Created.* A created status means that line items can be added and data maintained on a transfer order.
- *Shipped.* All lines have been shipped.
- *Received.* All lines have been received. Information cannot be changed for transfer orders with a shipped or received status.

- Each line item on a transfer order has a remaining status, as described below. This status is not shown in Figure 9.2 in order to keep the diagram simple.
- *Shipping Updates.* The line has only been created or the line has not been completely shipped.
- *Receive Updates.* The line has been completely shipped but not yet completely received.
- *Nothing.* The line has been completely shipped and received.

The inventory status for the item on a transfer order line is shown on the right side of Figure 9.2, where the inventory status varies for the different warehouses involved in the transfer. With respect to the ship-from warehouse, for example, the steps in transfer order processing will change the status from *On Order* to *Reserved Physical, Picked, Deducted* and *Sold.*

9.2 Key Considerations for Transfer Order Processing

Several aspects of AX functionality represent key considerations which build on the basic model of transfer order processing.

Significance of a Single Transfer Order A single transfer order usually represents a single shipment and the line items reflect the shipment contents. It sometimes represents a container with a unique identifier, and the transfer order number can be manually assigned to reflect the container identifier.

Shipment and Delivery Dates for a Transfer Order The transfer order header specifies a shipment date and receipt date, along with the ship-from and ship-to site/warehouses and a mode of delivery such as air or truck. The difference between the two dates reflects the expected transportation time (expressed in days) between the two locations.

The assignment of these dates is affected by the delivery date control policy assigned to the transfer order header, which can enforce basic rules such as the working calendar for both warehouses, the calendar for the delivery mode, and the expected transportation time between a pair of warehouses.

A delivery date control policy is also assigned to each transfer order line. It is inherited from the item based on its companywide or site-specific order settings (for transfer orders), much like an item's delivery date control policy (for sales orders) is inherited by a sales line. Figure 9.3 summarizes the delivery date control options for a transfer order line, and the significance of each option.

Figure 9.3 Delivery Date Control Options for a Transfer Order Line

Delivery Date Control Option	Scenario	Comments
Sales Lead Time	Use Basic Rules	Enforce basic rules for assignment of dates
ATP	Stocked Item	Enforce basic rules and use ATP logic for dates
None	Allow assignment of unrealistic dates	Ignore basic rules for assignment of dates

Transportation Time between Warehouses The transportation time between a pair of warehouses can be defined. The transportation time is expressed in days, and you can optionally specify a different number of days for different modes of delivery.

In certain special cases, the transportation time between warehouses will vary by item, such as a very large item that requires special transportation arrangements and a longer time for moving the item via large trucks. You can define this transfer time as part of the item's site/warehouse-specific coverage planning data.

Tracking Number for a Transfer Order You can optionally specify a tracking number for a transfer order and print an associated document (titled the Transfer Order Shipment) to accompany the transferred material.

One-Step Shipment for a Transfer Order Some scenarios employ a one-step shipment process for a transfer order, which means there is no tracking of in-transit inventory and no receipt transaction. You indicate this policy (termed the auto-receive policy) when posting a transfer order shipment. The one-step approach can be used with short transportation times.

Reserving Material for a Transfer Order Line Many scenarios employ reservations at the time you release a transfer order for picking, and the picking list (or picking work) communicates these reservations. Some scenarios require reservations at the time of creating a transfer order, and the reservation policy assigned to a transfer order line item indicates whether inventory will be reserved automatically or manually. When initially adding a line item, this policy – labeled Reserve Items Automatically -- is inherited from the transfer order header, and it can be overridden. The policy for the transfer order header can be inherited from a companywide policy (embedded in the Inventory and Warehouse Management parameters).

The reservation logic differs between the basic and advanced approaches to warehouse management. The advanced approach requires assignment of an additional item policy termed the reservation hierarchy.

Cost Change Variances on Transfers between AX Sites With a standard cost item, the item's site-specific standard costs can differ between two AX sites. The difference frequently reflects a higher standard cost at the ship-to site because of freight or other landed costs. Transferring the item will result in a cost change variance when the costs differ between two AX sites, where the variance is generated upon receipt at the ship-to site.

9.3 Coordinate Transfer Order Activities

A firm's S&OP game plans provide the primary driver of transfers for material items. The key tools for coordinating these activities include planned transfer orders and action messages, which reflect the model of SCM decision-making embedded in coverage planning data for transfers (Section 5.5). Other coordination tools include the visibility of needed picking/shipping and expected receiving for transfer orders.

Planned Transfer Orders The planned orders can be viewed on the Planned Transfer Orders form or the Planned Orders form, where the displayed information typically represents the current master plan.[2] A planned transfer order identifies the item's preferred refilling warehouse. You can also manually add a planned transfer order.

Actual transfer orders can be created from planned orders via a function termed *firming planned orders*. You typically mark (via a check box) the planned orders needing to be firmed. The firming function creates single-line transfer orders

---

[2] You can view information based on a selected set of master plan data or forecast plan data. For simplicity's sake the explanation focuses on the set of data representing the current master plan.

unless you indicate grouping preferences via the firming dialogue, such as grouping by a daily or weekly period size. Execution of the firming function automatically deletes the selected planned orders, and creates a log for tracking which planned orders have been firmed and by whom.

In many cases, you may need to analyze the rationale for a planned transfer order prior to firming. You can view the net requirements and related action messages for a selected planned order. The analysis may lead to one or more of the following actions. For example, you may change the suggested quantity or dates, or the ship-from warehouse,

Action Messages Action messages represent one of the key tools for coordinating transfer order activities to meet the S&OP game plans. Master scheduling logic can generate action messages for planned and actual transfer orders. The logic reflects the action message policies embedded within the coverage group assigned to an item, as described in a previous chapter (Section 5.8). The action messages can be viewed and acted upon in several different ways. For example, you can view the action messages on the Actions form, and optionally apply the suggested action for a selected message by accessing the Action Graph.

Messages about Calculated Delays This message indicates that a transfer order delivery date will cause a delay in meeting a requirement date, and the transfer order typically has an associated "advance" action message. The messages can be viewed from several starting points (such as the Net Requirements inquiry) and you can access the relevant order to indicate a change.

Other Coordination Tools for Transfer Orders Other coordination tools provide visibility of picking and receiving activities, and the tools vary when using the basic versus advanced approach to warehouse management. With the basic approach, for example, you can anticipate picking activities using the Release Transfer Order Picking form, and anticipate arrivals using the Arrival Overview form. With the advanced approach, you can anticipate picking activities using the Release to Warehouse form or the Load Planning Workbench.

9.4 Additional Case Studies

Case 9.1: Report a "Lost in Transit" Quantity for a Transfer Order

The receiving clerks can optionally identify that a scrap quantity applies to the received quantity. The scrap quantity may reflect material that has been lost in transit or scrapped material at the time of receipt. For example, a scrap quantity of 5 for the received quantity of 100 would result in an on-hand inventory of 95.

The scrap quantity automatically creates two transactions to add and subtract the inventory.

Case 9.2: Transfer Orders to/from a Subcontractor As part of subcontracted production, transfer orders were used to send the supplied material to the subcontractor warehouse and also transfer the finished quantities back to an internal warehouse. The actual receipt of a transfer order at the subcontractor was entered as a simple inventory transaction. A simple inventory transaction was also entered for actual shipment of a transfer order from the subcontractor.

9.5 Executive Summary

This chapter focused on transfer orders for coordinating transfers between inventory locations in a single company. It started with a basic model of transfer order processing and related life cycles, and the basic model provided a foundation for explaining key considerations and coordination of transfer orders.

Chapter 10

Inventory and Warehouse Management

Inventory and warehouse management involve the physical storage and movement of products within and between physical sites, as well as handling outbound and inbound shipments with trading partners. Various terms refer to these activities, and the responsibilities may be assigned to different roles within one or several functional areas. This book primarily uses the term warehouse management, and the typical roles include the warehouse manager, warehouse planner and warehouse worker. Other roles include receiving clerks, shipping clerks and transportation coordinators.

Many aspects of inventory and warehouse management have already been covered in previous chapters. For example, several fundamentals for modeling inventory locations were introduced at the beginning of the book, which explained the use of AX sites and AX warehouses to identify inventory locations. Subsequent chapters identified the applicability of these inventory locations in the definition of items, product costing, and coverage planning data.

One of the fundamentals for modeling inventory locations involves the choice of a warehouse management option, where the choice can be warehouse-specific. The two major options consist of a basic approach and an advanced approach to warehouse management, and they represent two different conceptual models for managing inventory and related business processes. The impact on business processes were covered in previous chapters about sales orders, purchase orders and transfer orders. This chapter summarizes the two options and the significance of Inventory Status. It also explains the AX viewpoint of inventory transactions and the workspaces related to inventory and warehouse management. These considerations are reflected in the following sections within the chapter.

1. Strategic Options for Warehouse Management
2. Significance of Inventory Status
3. Basic Approach to Warehouse Management
4. Advanced Approach to Warehouse Management
5. AX Viewpoint of Inventory Transactions
6. Workspaces Related to Inventory and Warehouse Management
7. Additional Case Studies

10.1 Strategic Options for Warehouse Management

Dynamics AX supports a range of options for warehouse management capabilities, but the options can be broadly grouped into a basic approach and an advanced approach. The choice of an approach can be warehouse-specific, so that a company may use the advanced approach at some warehouses and the basic approach at other warehouses. The two approaches share a high degree of common functionality, but the advanced approach has a much broader amount of functionality and supports out-of-the-box mobile device transactions. Both approaches can optionally take advantage of capabilities related to Inventory Status.

This section reviews the two major options for warehouse management and the applicability of Inventory Status. It also provides some guidelines for choosing an option.

Major Options for Warehouse Management The various warehouse management options have been called many different names, but they boil down to two major options. For simplicity's sake, one major option can be termed the "Basic Inventory approach" or the "basic approach" for short. The second major option can be termed the "Advanced WMS approach" or the "advanced approach" for short. The two options have also been called "WMS I" and "WHS".

The two major options are differentiated by a warehouse policy and an item-related policy about "use warehouse management processes." The advanced approach only applies to warehouse transactions for a WMS-enabled item at a WMS-enabled warehouse, whereas the basic approach applies to the other combinations of these two policies. Figure 10.1 summarizes these key policies and the two major options for warehouse management, identified as Option #1 and #2. It also identifies the terminology about items and warehouses, such as a WMS-enabled item, a WMS-enabled warehouse and a non-WMS warehouse.

Figure 10.1 Major Options for Warehouse Management

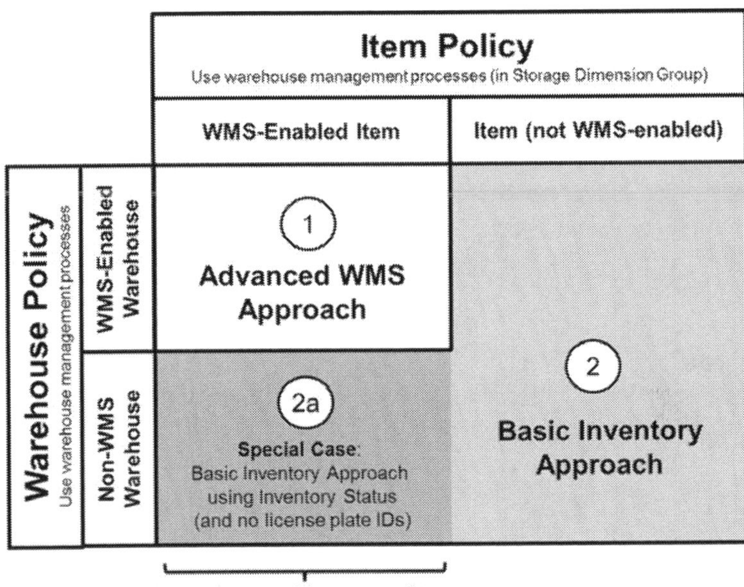

The two major options are also reflected in the AX user documentation, which differentiates various topics as applicable to "features in the warehouse management module" versus "features in the inventory management module." Each option has some unique constructs and functionality, but the two major options also share a high degree of common functionality. For those already familiar with previous AX versions, you already know most of the functionality associated with the basic approach based on your experience with the historical "WMS I" capabilities.

Applicability of Inventory Status The capabilities related to Inventory Status only apply to WMS-enabled items. It always applies to the advanced approach, and it represents a special case for the basic approach -- identified as Option #2a in Figure 10.1. The significance of Inventory Status is largely determined by user-defined values, and most scenarios employ at least two values. One value typically indicates good inventory, such as a value of *Available* or *Good*. One or more values can be designated as blocked in order to prevent usage of inventory with the assigned value, and master scheduling logic treats inventory with a blocked value as non-nettable. Examples of these blocked values include *Damaged* or *To-Be-Scrapped*. The next section provides further explanation about the significance of Inventory Status.

Guidelines for choosing the Basic vs Advanced Approach As a general guideline, the advanced approach typically applies to those warehouses that require tracking of palletized inventory (identified by license plate IDs), more sophisticated capabilities to support warehouse/transportation requirements, and out-of-the-box functionality for mobile devices, especially when warehouse users need guidance about finding or placing inventory. However, the advanced approach also supports scenarios that do not employ license plate tracking in their inventory locations, and the use of license plate IDs is largely hidden from end-users. The more sophisticated capabilities to support warehouse and transportation requirements are sometimes a leading indicator for choosing the advanced approach.

The basic approach typically applies to a warehouse (or company) that does not have sophisticated requirements for sales order picking/shipping, and does not require tracking of palletized inventory. Inventory within the warehouse is typically tracked by piece rather than by pallet. In addition, the basic approach does not support out-of-the box mobile device transactions, although third-party applications can be used. The basic approach supports simple order-based picking for sales orders and transfer orders, and also supports the wave picking concept for these orders.

Evolving Strategies for Strategic Options An evolving strategy can help reduce the complexity and cost of the initial phase of an ERP implementation. The flexibility to evolve can be considered within each of the two major approaches, and from one approach to the other. As one example of an evolving strategy within the Advanced WMS approach, a given warehouse may start with the simplest use of mobile device transactions and the advanced functionality and then evolve to fully utilize them and to fully use the advanced transportation management capabilities.

As an example for the Basic Inventory approach, a given warehouse may start with the basic approach as an interim step to the advanced approach. Even when the primary warehouses employ the advanced approach, the basic approach is typically required for managing inventory at off-site warehouses such as subcontractors or smaller locations.

10.2 Significance of Inventory Status

The significance of Inventory Status is largely determined by user-defined values, and it only applies to WMS-enabled items. Most scenarios employ at least two user-defined values. One value typically indicates good inventory, such as a value of *Available* or *Good.* One or more values can be defined and designated as blocked in order to prevent usage of inventory with the assigned value, and master scheduling logic treats inventory with a blocked value as non-nettable. Examples of these blocked values include *Blocked, Damaged* or *To-Be-Scrapped.*

You define the possible values of Inventory Status, and a value must be assigned to all orders (such as sales order lines and to all supply orders) and inventory transactions. Several characteristics are particularly important for warehouse and quality management purposes, such as the ability to assign a different value during the receiving process, the different approaches of changing the value for existing inventory, and the allowable transactions for existing inventory with a value representing a blocked status. These considerations are reflected in the following topics within the section

- Two Different Meanings of the term Inventory Status
- Define the Values for Inventory Status
- Assign a Value for Inventory Status to Orders
- Default Values for Modeling a Purchased Item's Inspection Requirements
- Ability to Override a Value for Inventory Status during the Receiving Process
- Ability to Change the Value for Inventory Status for Existing Inventory
- Allowable Transactions for Inventory with a Blocked Inventory Status

Two Different Meanings of the term Inventory Status The term "inventory status" has many different meanings in different ERP systems. It has two different meanings in AX. As the primary focus, Inventory Status refers to one of the mandatory dimensions within a Storage Group Dimension that has been enabled to "use warehouse management processes." Related policies indicate whether a value for Inventory Status should be considered for sales pricing, purchase pricing, and/or coverage planning purposes. An additional consideration applies when using the advanced approach to warehouse management, since Inventory Status must be designated in the reservation hierarchy as critical or simply informational for reservation purposes.

The term "inventory status" also refers to the AX viewpoint of inventory transactions, where the status indicates steps in the life cycle of orders for an item. The system-assigned values of an inventory status differ for each type of order. For example, the applicable values for a purchase order line indicate whether the item has been *Ordered*, *Received* or *Purchased*, and the status is automatically updated by different steps in the business process. A subsequent section describes the AX viewpoint of inventory transactions (Section 10.5).

In order to differentiate the two different meanings, this book employs capital letters (for Inventory Status) and lower case letters (for inventory status) for the same term, although the context of the term usually provides sufficient clues about its meaning.

Define the Values for Inventory Status You create a user-defined value and name using the Inventory Status form. One value typically indicates good inventory, such as a user-defined value of *Available* or *Good.* One or more values can be defined and designated as blocked in order to prevent usage of inventory with the assigned value. Master scheduling logic considers the inventory with a blocked value to be non-nettable; it is assumed the inventory cannot be used.

Assign a Value for Inventory Status to Orders A value for Inventory Status must be entered for every type of order. This includes line items on purchase orders, transfer orders and sales orders, as well as production orders and the related lines in a Production BOM. A value is also required on basic inventory transactions. The use of default values for Inventory Status can help streamline data entry, especially for modeling a normal business. The use of default values can also reflect different purposes of Inventory Status.

For most scenarios, a default value of *Available* or its equivalent should be assigned as a companywide policy, and as the default for every site and warehouse involved in normal business. In this way, every transaction will inherit the value unless a different source of the default value applies. For example, the default value for an item can model an item's inspection requirements.

Default Values for Modeling a Purchased Item's Inspection Requirements As one purpose of Inventory Status, it can provide the basis for identifying needed inspection of purchase order receipts. For example, a value of *Needs-Inspection* can be assigned to a purchase order line item so that it is identified when reporting purchase order arrival. A given item that always requires inspection can be assigned a default value of *Needs-Inspection* using the Default Item Status form. In this way, the value will be inherited when creating a purchase order line or firming a planned order.

Ability to Override a Value for Inventory Status during the Receiving Process The ability to override a value for Inventory Status during the receiving process applies to all types of orders except transfer orders. This includes the receiving process for purchase orders, RMAs and production orders.

For example, the value of *Available* for a purchase order line can be overridden when reporting arrival, such as changing the value to *Needs-Inspection*, *Return-to-Vendor* or *To-Be-Scrapped*.

The use of automatically-created quality orders may influence how you assign a value during the receiving process. As an additional consideration, you can indicate a scrapped quantity when reporting the finished quantity for a production order, or when reporting receipt of a transfer order line. The value can also be assigned for additions to inventory via inventory adjustments, quantity adjustments or cycle counts.

Ability to Change the Value for Inventory Status for Existing Inventory Several approaches can change the value of Inventory Status. The value can be changed using a mobile device transaction, or using the forms titled Warehouse Inventory Status Change and Change Inventory Status. One form changes status for selected existing inventory with a specified status, and the other form changes status for all existing inventory at a selected location.

A rework order can be used to change the value of Inventory Status. For example, an item's inventory may be assigned an unblocked status of *Needs-Rework*, and you can create a rework order in order to change the status to *Available*.

A quality order can be used to change the value of Inventory Status based on the test results. The quality order can be manually or automatically generated, and the material being tested can have a blocked or unblocked status. As part of the quality order information, you specify the associated value for "fail" and another value for "pass", so that validation of the test results will automatically change the status.

Allowable Transactions for Inventory with a Blocked Inventory Status The allowable transactions include purchase order returns, inventory adjustments, cycle counts, inventory transfers and quality orders. Otherwise, a blocked value prevents inventory transactions.

10.3 Basic Approach to Warehouse Management

A summary of the basic approach to warehouse management includes a few fundamentals and the business processes for different warehouse transactions.

Fundamentals of the Basic Approach The fundamentals include the definition of warehouse locations and the use of basic inventory transactions. As part of the setup information for a non-WMS warehouse, you define bin locations within the warehouse and a few item-related policies. The basic inventory transactions include movements between inventory locations (via the Transfer Journal), adjustments (via the Inventory Adjustment Journal or Quantity Adjustments), and physical counts (via the Counting Journal).

Sales Order Picking/Shipping A typical process was previously described as part of the basic model of sales order processing (Section 7.1).

Purchase Order Receiving A typical process was previously described as part of the basic model of purchase order processing (Section 8.1).

Transfer Order Picking/Shipping and Receiving The typical processes were previously described as part of the basic model of transfer order processing (Section 9.1).

10.4 Advanced Approach to Warehouse Management

A summary of the advanced approach to warehouse management includes a few fundamentals and the business processes for different warehouse transactions. The advanced approach supports multiple variations for each business process, but these fall outside the scope of this essential guide. The related use of license plates and work orders are also summarized.

Fundamentals of the Advanced Approach The fundamentals include the setup information about warehouse locations, item-related policies, and mobile device transactions The fundamentals also include the use of basic inventory transactions such as inventory adjustments and moves..

Overview of License Plates A license plate can represent a physical entity or a logical entity. The significance of a license plate is easiest to conceptualize in terms of a physical pallet, where a standard quantity of the same item is typically placed on a pallet, and a license plate identifier has been assigned to the pallet. The license plate ID provides a convenient way to view inventory balances by pallet, and to report receipts, movement and picking. The concept of a license plate applies to many scenarios, and license plate tracking must be designated for applicable bin locations. However, some scenarios do not want or need license plate tracking, so that applicable bin locations are not enabled for license plate tracking.

Overview of Work Orders Work orders support many different types of warehouse transactions -- ranging from sales order picking to putaway of purchase order arrivals -- and there are different ways to create a work order. For example, some work orders are created by mobile device transactions and other work orders are created by client transactions. The execution of a work order is typically reported via a mobile device transaction. The ability to create and execute work orders via a mobile device transaction requires definition of the corresponding mobile device menu items.

A work order consists of a header and multiple work lines which represent a set of interrelated warehouse activities identified by a Work ID. You enter or scan the Work ID when reporting various mobile device transactions for a work order. The execution of a work order creates entries for inventory transaction history. When viewing transaction history, a transaction filter can limit the displayed information to "work only" transactions or "omit work" transactions, or you can view "display all" transactions. The "work only" transactions identify the related work order.

Sales Order Picking/Shipping A typical process for an order-based picking/shipping approach was previously described as part of the basic model of sales order processing (Section 7.1). The advanced approach supports other variations of sales order picking/shipping. These include variations of the release to warehouse step, wave picking, load planning, manual or automated packing, replenishment of picking locations, and staging/loading steps. However, further explanation falls outside the scope of this essential guide.

Purchase Order Receiving A typical process was previously described as part of the basic model of purchase order processing (Section 8.1).

Transfer Order Picking/Shipping and Receiving A typical process was previously described as part of the basic model of transfer order processing (Section 9.1). The advanced approach supports other variations of transfer order picking/shipping. These include variations of the release to warehouse step, wave picking, load planning, and staging/loading steps. However, further explanation falls outside the scope of this essential guide.

Cycle Counting The advanced approach to warehouse management supports several options for cycle counting. One option involves the use of a cycle count plan for a complete physical inventory or for cycle count purposes. A second option supports the ad hoc generation of a cycle count for selected items or locations. The third option involves cycle counting as part of the sales order picking process, so that cycle count work will be automatically created when picking reduces an item's inventory below a specified quantity (aka the cycle counting threshold). Each option generates work orders for counting, and the warehouse worker uses the mobile device to report completion of the picking work. A mobile device transaction also supports a spot count. Cycle counting discrepancies may occur in each variation, which requires a separate process to resolve a discrepancy.

10.5 AX Viewpoint of Inventory Transactions

A key aspect of understanding AX involves the viewpoint of inventory transactions and the associated inventory status. Dynamics AX employs a broader viewpoint of the term inventory transaction since it reflects both actual and anticipated receipts and issues. Additional types of inventory transactions related to work orders are also employed by the Advanced WMS approach to warehouse management.

AX Viewpoint of Inventory Transactions The term inventory transaction normally refers to the actual physical movement of material, such as an inventory adjustment, receipt or shipment. Dynamics AX employs a broader viewpoint because it reflects both actual and anticipated receipts and issues. With orders, for example, it creates an inventory transaction with an associated inventory status that reflects various steps in order processing. Previous chapters illustrated the values of inventory status in the typical business process for sales orders (Section 7.1), purchase orders (Section 8.1), and transfer orders (Section 9.1).

Impact of Work Orders on Inventory Transaction History The Advanced WMS approach to warehouse management employs different types of work orders. The execution of a work order creates entries for inventory transaction history. When viewing transaction history, a transaction filter can limit the displayed information to just the work order transactions or just the normal inventory transactions. The "work only" transactions identify the related work order, whereas normal inventory transactions identify the related sales order, purchase order, transfer order, production order or inventory journal.

10.6 Workspaces Related to Inventory and Warehouse Management

Several predefined workspaces are related to inventory and warehouse management, as described in the following summary of each workspace and its applicable functionality.

Cost Administration Workspace This workspace includes links to key reports/inquiries about inventory accounting, such as inventory value statements, inventory aging, standard cost transactions, and calculation of ABC classifications.

Cost Analysis Workspace This workspace summarizes inventory turns and inventory accuracy (with drill down to those items with low turns or accuracy) as well as inventory value (with segmentation by item group and also total inventory value over time). The links provide access to key reports/inquiries about inventory accounting, such as inventory value statements, inventory aging, and calculation of ABC classifications.

Outbound Work Planning Workspace This workspace summarizes several aspects of the Advanced WMS approach to sales order picking/shipping as well as transfer order picking/shipping. For example, you can perform the periodic task for automatic release of sales orders or transfer orders. The links provide access to related information such as shipments, waves, and work.

Outbound Work Monitoring Workspace This workspace summarizes several aspects of the Advanced WMS approach to replenishment of picking lines. For a selected warehouse, it identifies the active replenishment work for shipment waves and the unreleased replenishment work. The links provide access to other types of work orders (such as cycle count work, sales order picking work, transfer order picking work, and inventory movement work), and to information about the shipments (or loads) at a packing station.

10.7 Additional Case Studies

Case 10.1: Identify Off-Spec or Blemished Products using Inventory Status A sporting goods company occasionally had off-spec or blemished products that could be sold at a reduced price. They defined a value of "Off-Spec" for Inventory Status, and assigned the "Off-Spec" value to finished goods when applicable. They also defined lower sales prices in their sales price trade agreements for items with an Inventory Status of "Off-Spec." On the occasion, off-spec products were also purchased for their distribution warehouse, and they similarly used purchase price agreements.

Case 10.2: Correcting Errors about Purchase Order Receipts The receiving clerks would sometimes make a mistake in the reported quantity received. In order to correct the mistake, the supervisor would access the Product Receipt Journal form and select the "Correct" function to access the Product Receipt Correction form. The supervisor would enter the correct quantity for the relevant line and select a reason code for the correction. In this way, the inventory balances and financial information would reflect the correction.

Case 10.3: Expedite Policies for Sales Order Picking The customer service reps at a manufacturing/distribution company used several different approaches to indicate the need for expediting when entering a sales order. As the starting point, the assignment of shipment and delivery dates reflected available to promise logic so that unrealistic dates would not be assigned. The customer service reps assigned an expedited mode of delivery which also resulted in the automatic assignment of a expedite code. The shipping clerks would use this expedite code and mode of delivery to help prioritize the generation of picking lists (or the sales order picking work) and ultimately provide expedited service.

Case 10.4: Putaway Logic based on Zones Within a Warehouse As part of the advanced approach to warehouse management, the warehouse manager defined different zones (and the related locations within each zone) to support putaway logic about an item's storage requirements. Examples of a zone included the *cooler* room and a *toxic* product area. In addition, the storage requirements for relevant items were identified by the assignment of a filter code value to the item (such as the user-defined values of *cooler* or *toxic*). A location directive about the relevant putaway zone could then be based on the item characteristic.

10.8 Executive Summary

Inventory and warehouse management involve the physical storage and movement of products within and between inventory locations, as well as handling outbound and inbound shipments with trading partners. One of the fundamentals of modeling inventory locations within AX involves the choice between the basic versus advanced approach to warehouse management, and the choice can be warehouse specific. The two options represent different conceptual models for managing inventory and related business processes, although both options share a high degree of common functionality and can support the Inventory Status capabilities.

This chapter summarized the two major options for warehouse management. It also provided more detailed explanations about the significance of Inventory Status, and summarized the AX viewpoint of inventory transactions and the workspaces related to inventory and warehouse management.

Chapter 11

Basics of Quality Management

The concerns of quality management typically extend across every aspect of supply chain management. This broad viewpoint ranges from the definition of item and product structure information through sourcing purchased material, actual production, sales shipments, and returns. A narrower viewpoint focuses on several aspects of unique functionality for quality management. As an Essential Guide, this chapter focuses on two key aspects about inventory blocking and cases, and consists of the following sections.

1. Summary of Inventory Blocking Approaches
2. Using Cases for Quality Purposes

11.1 Summary of Inventory Blocking Approaches

Inventory blocking represents a key tool for quality management, such as preventing usage and indicating the need for inspection. There are three basic sources or approaches for inventory blocking -- labeled Inventory Status, Quality Order and Manual. Each approach results in an entry on the Inventory Blocking form along with information about the source of blocking. This information can act as a coordination tool for quality management.

One approach employs a blocked value for Inventory Status, as described in a previous chapter (Section 10.2). The second approach employs quality orders, and often works in conjunction with the values of Inventory Status. The third approach involves manual assignment of inventory blocking. The three approaches differ in how the inventory blocking is created and removed, their impact on master scheduling logic, and their allowable transactions. The three approaches are summarized in Figure 11.1 and described below.

Figure 11.1 Summary of Inventory Blocking Approaches

Considerations about Blocking	Type of Inventory Blocking		
	Inventory Status	Quality Order	Manual
Create blocking for the specified inventory of item	Assign a blocked value for Inventory Status	Create a quality order with full blocking	Manually assign inventory blocking
Ability to assign blocking at time of order receipt	Yes	Yes	No
Remove blocking	Change a blocked value for Inventory Status	Delete or complete the quality order	Delete manual assignment of inventory blocking
Impact of blocked inventory on master scheduling logic	Non-nettable	Nettable on expected date	Non-nettable or Nettable on expected date
Allowable transactions for the blocked inventory	Move, adjustment out Cycle count Return to vendor Create quality order	None	None
Description for blocking	None	Yes	Yes
Note/document for blocking	None	Yes	Yes
Additional considerations	Assign to subset of a batch number Different ways to change value of Inventory Status	Block just sample quantity Impact next steps for order Destructive testing Update Inventory Status or Batch Disposition Code	Assign to subset of a batch number

Inventory Blocking based on a blocked value of Inventory Status This approach reflects a blocked value for Inventory Status which can be assigned at the time of order receipt. The blocking can be viewed on the Inventory Blocking form, and it can only be removed by changing it to a non-blocked value. The inventory is treated as unusable and non-nettable by master scheduling logic. The blocking prevents most inventory transactions with the exception of moves, adjustments, cycle counts, returns to vendor and creation of a quality order. A blocked value can be changed by a quality order or changed directly (via a client or mobile device transaction). A blocked value can also be assigned to a subset of a batch number or to a specific serial number.

Inventory Blocking based on a Quality Order This approach reflects a quality order with "full blocking" as part of the policies for item sampling. A quality order can be manually created for the specified inventory of an item, including inventory that has already been assigned a blocked value for Inventory Status. Alternatively, an item's quality order can be automatically created based on policies defined on the Quality Association form, such as automatic creation as a result of reporting purchase order arrival or the finished quantity for a production order. Using the Inventory Blocking form, you can optionally define a description and/or notes about blocking related to a quality order.

With full blocking, the inventory associated with a quality order is treated by master scheduling logic as nettable with an expected availability date. This expected outcome is indicated by the automatically-assigned Expected Receipts checkbox. The expected date inherits the creation date and can be manually changed. However, the blocking prevents all inventory transactions.

Blocking based on a quality order has several additional considerations shown at the bottom of Figure 11.1. For example, blocking can just apply to a small sample quantity, and a quality order can be used to update the value of Inventory Status or the Batch Disposition Code.

Inventory Blocking based on Manual Assignment This approach reflects a manual assignment of inventory blocking to existing inventory. It can only be created and deleted on the Inventory Blocking form, and you can optionally define a description and/or notes about the manual blocking. When you create manual blocking, you can indicate the expected outcome as non-nettable or as nettable with an expected availability date. You indicate the expected outcome via an Expected Receipts checkbox. The expected date inherits the creation date and can be manually changed. Manual blocking prevents all inventory transactions. For example, the manual blocking must be removed in order to report the inventory as scrapped. Manual blocking can also be assigned to a subset of a batch number or to a specific serial number.

11.2 Using Cases for Quality Purposes

A quality issue can be identified by a case, and case management provides a multi-faceted approach to manage issues raised by customers, vendors or employees. Each case is uniquely identified by a Case ID. At its simplest, you manually create a case and a description, and then indicate progress (via the case status of opened, in-process, and closed or cancelled) and case resolution (of accept, reject or none). The optional facets of case management serve several different purposes and involve different types of setup information, as illustrated by the following.

- *Case Category*. A user-defined hierarchy of case categories will reflect the types of issues in a given business situation, and you must assign a case category to each case. As a simple example, the top of one hierarchy may be labeled sales, and consist of several case categories related to sales and customer service issues. For each case category, you can optionally define additional information about the need for creating an activity such as a task, action, event or appointment. You can also identify an associated case process, as described in the next point.

- *Case Process.* A user-defined case process identifies the steps to follow when working on a case. A step can be required or optional. Each step can optionally have a specified activity, priority and responsibility. Linking a case process to a case category enables you to standardize your business processes for different types of issues.

- *Case Details about the Associated Customer, Item or Sales Order.* One or more associations can be defined for a case. In the context of sales, for example, the association may reflect a customer, item or sales order, or even a lead, opportunity, prospect or project. The association may reflect a vendor, item, purchase order or invoice in the context of purchasing.

Additional facets of case management have other applications. For example, cases can be automatically created to identify audit violations based on audit policies (such as an invoice from a certain vendor), and a product change case can support changes to the BOM version or route version for a manufactured item.

11.3 Additional Case Studies

Case 11.1: Certificates of Analysis for Sales Order Shipments A manufacturer enclosed a certificate of analysis with sales order shipments of selected items. The certificate reflected the test results reported for the item, where test results were captured as part of a quality order. The contents of a certificate of analysis reflected each customer's requirements for selected test results.

Case 11.2: Nonconformance Reports for Purchased Material When a problem was identified, a quality specialist created a nonconformance report that identified the problem source and assigned a user-definable problem type. If it was approved for further action, it was assigned one or more corrective actions that identified what type of diagnostic should be performed, who should perform it, and the requested date for completion.

11.4 Executive Summary

This chapter summarized two key aspects of quality management. One aspect involved the different approaches to inventory blocking, such as the use of Inventory Status and quality orders. The other aspect involved the use of cases for quality management purposes, such as customer complaints or problems with purchased material. The case studies included certificates of analysis for sales order shipments and nonconformance reports for purchased material.

Chapter 12

Summary

This book focused on how Microsoft Dynamics AX provides an integrated ERP system to support supply chain management in manufacturing and distribution. The targeted reader consists of SCM professionals that need to initially learn AX. It provided an overview of the essential business processes and capabilities, and presented a linear sequence of topics that build on each other. It covered the embedded conceptual models and business processes that ultimately shape your vocabulary for describing system usage.

The linear sequence of topics started with the fundamentals of modeling inventory locations and the definition of material items, including the basics of product costing. The sequence continued with the definition of coverage planning data to model SCM decision-making, and an overview of S&OP game plans and the use of master scheduling logic to coordinate supply chain activities. Subsequent chapters covered the key business processes related to sales orders, purchase orders, and transfer orders, and some basic aspects of warehouse management and quality management. Many of the chapters included Business Process Modeling (BPM) diagrams about basic business processes, and these provided the foundation covering major variations. Case studies illustrated how the AX software functionality applies to many different scenarios in manufacturing and distribution.

As an Essential Guide, it represents an abbreviated version of my complete book for "Supply Chain Management using Microsoft Dynamics AX: 2016 Edition". It focused on topics that apply to both distribution and manufacturing, but skimmed over the manufacturing-related topics due to book length considerations. These topics are covered in the complete book.

The book contents covered the two major options currently available for using AX, which can be labeled "Dynamics AX 2012 R3" and the "new Dynamics AX". The two options provide the same supply chain management functionality with some slight differences, so that the book contents apply to both options.

The book identified the slight differences such as the variations in user experience and the workspace capabilities.

Concluding Remarks When learning any ERP software package, it is important to understand its underlying conceptual models and how it supports basic business processes and their variations. It is easy to get bogged down in the navigational details. This book summarized how Microsoft Dynamics AX can support supply chain management in manufacturing and distribution businesses, and addressed the learning objectives for those new to AX.

Appendix A
Scope of Book Topics and Prior Research

The book focuses on supply chain management topics for distribution and manufacturing companies, and this focus guided the prior research and the scope of book topics.

Prior Research Several steps of prior research were undertaken to understand the supply chain management requirements in manufacturing/distribution, and the AX functionality to support those requirements. With respect to AX 2012 R3 (as well as previous AX versions), these steps included participation in training classes, webinars, and conference sessions; reviews of the existing training materials, e-learning lessons, user documentation and sales demo materials; reviews of blogs and articles; discussions with users, development personnel, and field consultants; and hands-on testing for thousands of use cases that reflected common requirements in manufacturing and distribution. With few exceptions, only those capabilities personally tested and proven were included in the book contents.[1] The same approach was also undertaken for my previous books about Dynamics AX. The discussions with experienced field consultants helped identify the dominant business practices at current users. On-going opportunities to consult with current users have supplemented this understanding.

The prior research concerning the new Dynamics AX has been following similar steps. This included participation in pre-release webinars and conferences, discussions with leading experts and Microsoft team members, reading the currently available information, and hands-on testing of hundreds of use cases. These same use cases were previously tested for AX 2012 R3, thereby supporting

[1] The prior research and hands-on testing for AX 2012 R3 reflect the software capabilities through the CU9 release.

a comparative analysis of the two options. The book contents reflect my prior research up until the beginning of the year 2016.

The prior research about SCM requirements included my consulting and teaching experiences with manufacturing and distribution firms across the past three decades. These experiences included responses to numerous RFPs (requests for proposal) for an ERP system, face-to-face consulting engagements with several hundred firms, and teaching executive seminars, APICS certification classes, MBA courses, and user group sessions. My understanding is continually being supplemented by staying abreast of the current literature and discussions with various thought leaders about using ERP systems.

Scope of Book Topics The book topics focus on supply chain management, and the selection of book topics was shaped by several factors. First, the selected topics excluded the integrated accounting applications -- such as payables, receivables, general ledger, payroll and human resources -- except for key intersection points with SCM. Second, several SCM-related topics were excluded because of book length considerations -- such as lean manufacturing, project-oriented operations, service-oriented operations and retail operations – although they are mentioned in several places. Each of these excluded topics merit a separate book, much like my separate books about warehouse management and process manufacturing. The excluded topic of non-stock purchases reflects the focus on material items. Third, a few topics were excluded because they could not be personally tested and proven within the budgeted time.

The book length considerations precluded screen shots.[2] Other important topics of system development and usage were also excluded, such as business intelligence, security, and customization capabilities within the AX development environment.

Contributions to the AX Body of Knowledge The body of knowledge related to Microsoft Dynamics AX consists of several levels and components. The foundation level consists of the software, documentation and training materials provided by Microsoft. Additional contributions to the AX body of knowledge build on this foundation. In terms of the book's contributions, I have attempted to summarize the relevant information with an integrative viewpoint of how the whole system fits together to support supply chain management -- especially in manufacturing and distribution businesses. The book explains the embedded conceptual models and business processes for running these businesses.

---

[2] One argument against screen shot examples is that many companies tailor the standard screens, and the displayed information is also affected by license key activation. .

List of Figures

List of Cases

About the Author

Scott Hamilton has specialized in SCM/ERP information systems for three decades and consulted globally with several hundred manufacturing/distribution companies. His publications include multiple books about SCM using Dynamics AX as well as two textbooks about SCM/ERP, and his books have been translated into Russian and Chinese. His regular column "The AX Solution Architect" is published in MSDynamicsWorld.com. Scott has been a frequent speaker at Microsoft and AXUG events around the world, and a multi-year winner of the rarely-given Microsoft MVP award for AX. He earned a doctorate in information systems specializing in manufacturing and taught SCM/ERP as an MBA professor at several leading universities in North America, Europe and the Pacific Rim. He lives in Minnesota, a place where people still build ice castles.

About UXC Eclipse

Scott Hamilton has become the “go to” authority on Microsoft Dynamics AX in the manufacturing space. His books provide valuable insights into the market place we serve, which gives us all the opportunity to expand our thinking and see beyond the software features and functions.

UXC Eclipse is widely recognized as a global leader in industry solutions built on the Dynamics AX platform. We have a depth of experience across the horizontal global ERP market with specific focus on industry solutions for Retail, Wholesale and Distribution, Manufacturing and the surrounding supply chain.

We help organizations streamline their business and operational processes to bring the best from their organizational experience to the best of our Dynamics AX solutions; the result is ‘win-win’. From their Dynamics AX solutions, our customers realize operational efficiencies, improve business performance and heighten their supply chain collaboration. At UXC Eclipse we use a combination of old-fashioned service with ISO-9001 accredited quality systems and controls to ensure our implementations deliver to our customers’ expectations – on time and on budget. Our happy customers are the true indication of our success. With a global team of over 650 people, some 2,700 customer sites rely on UXC Eclipse for their project implementation services and everyday support.

We trust you find this book to be a useful insight into Microsoft Dynamics AX. If UXC Eclipse can be of service on your supply chain journey, then please get in touch with us at *www.uxceclipse.com*

Bradley Stroop
Chief Executive Officer
UXC Eclipse Group

Made in the USA
Middletown, DE
17 May 2018